WEST-E Library Media
0310
Teacher Certification Exam

By: Sharon Wynne, M.S.
Southern Connecticut State University

"And, while there's no reason yet to panic, I think it's only prudent that we make preparations to panic."

XAMonline, INC.
Boston

Copyright © 2008 XAMonline, Inc.
All rights reserved. No part of the material protected by this copyright notice may be reproduced or utilized in any form or by any means, electronic or mechanical, including photocopying, recording or by any information storage and retrievable system, without written permission from the copyright holder.

To obtain permission(s) to use the material from this work for any purpose including workshops or seminars, please submit a written request to:

XAMonline, Inc.
21 Orient Ave.
Melrose, MA 02176
Toll Free 1-800-509-4128
Email: info@xamonline.com
Web www.xamonline.com
Fax: 1-781-662-9268

Library of Congress Cataloging-in-Publication Data

Wynne, Sharon A.
    Library Media 0310: Teacher Certification / Sharon A. Wynne. -2nd ed.
    ISBN 978-1-58197- 635-9
    1. Library Media 0310   2. Study Guides.   3. WEST
    4. Teachers' Certification & Licensure.   5. Careers

Disclaimer:
The opinions expressed in this publication are the sole works of XAMonline and were created independently from the National Education Association, Educational Testing Service, or any State Department of Education, National Evaluation Systems or other testing affiliates.

Between the time of publication and printing, state specific standards as well as testing formats and website information may change that is not included in part or in whole within this product. Sample test questions are developed by XAMonline and reflect similar content as on real tests; however, they are not former tests. XAMonline assembles content that aligns with state standards but makes no claims nor guarantees teacher candidates a passing score. Numerical scores are determined by testing companies such as NES or ETS and then are compared with individual state standards. A passing score varies from state to state.

Printed in the United States of America

WEST-E: Library Media 310
ISBN: 978-1-58197-635-9

TEACHER CERTIFICATION STUDY GUIDE

Table of Contents

COMPETENCY 1.0 PROGRAM ADMINISTRATION

Skill 1.1   Organization, administration, and evaluation of the library media center 1

Skill 1.2   Planning and evaluation 5

Skill 1.3   Management: budgeting, staffing, training, and supervising student aides and volunteers 11

Skill 1.4   Establishing policies and procedures 17

Skill 1.5   Renovating facilities and planning new facilities 21

COMPETENCY 2.0 COLLECTION DEVELOPMENT

Skill 2.1   Selection policy 25

Skill 2.2   Selecting resources 32

Skill 2.3   Selecting equipment, supplies, and services 35

Skill 2.4   Acquiring resources 36

Skill 2.5   Organizing resources 38

Skill 2.6   Promotion of resources 41

COMPETENCY 3.0 INFORMATION ACCESS AND DELIVERY

Skill 3.1   Knowledge of information resources 43

Skill 3.2   Knowledge of literature 46

Skill 3.3   Knowledge of current technologies 49

Skill 3.4   Knowledge of the information retrieval processes 52

Skill 3.5   Information resources sharing 54

Skill 3.6   Online resources and databases 56

Skill 3.7   Distance learning 57

Skill 3.8   Equal access for all learners 58

LIBRARY MEDIA

Skill 3.9	Scheduling	59
Skill 3.10	Library media center environment	60
Skill 3.11	Ethical and legal concerns surrounding use of information	60

COMPETENCY 4.0 LEARNING AND TEACHING

Skill 4.1	Curriculum integration and development	63
Skill 4.2	Collaborative teaching and planning	66
Skill 4.3	Knowledge of learning styles and developmental levels of students	69
Skill 4.4	Knowledge of teaching and assessment strategies	71
Skill 4.5	Orientation techniques	72
Skill 4.6	Knowledge of information literacy models and principles	73
Skill 4.7	Teaching use of information resources and search strategies	74

COMPETENCY 5.0 PROFESSIONAL DEVELOPMENT, LEADERSHIP, AND ADVOCACY

Skill 5.1	Professional development	77
Skill 5.2	Awareness of the role and function of professional organizations	78
Skill 5.3	Familiarity with professional resources	80
Skill 5.4	Community involvement	81
Skill 5.5	Codes of ethics	82
Skill 5.6	Awareness of issues and trends	83
Skill 5.7	Advocacy	84
Skill 5.8	Certification and accreditation	84
Skill 5.9	Legislation affecting libraries and education	85

TEACHER CERTIFICATION STUDY GUIDE

Resources 88

Sample Test 98

Answer Key 127

Rigor Table 128

Rationales with Sample Questions 129

Web Resources 179

TEACHER CERTIFICATION STUDY GUIDE

Great Study and Testing Tips!

What to study in order to prepare for the subject assessments is the focus of this study guide but equally important is *how* you study.

You can increase your chances of truly mastering the information by taking some simple, but effective steps.

Study Tips:

1. Some foods aid the learning process. Foods such as milk, nuts, seeds, rice, and oats help your study efforts by releasing natural memory enhancers called CCKs (*cholecystokinin*) composed of *tryptophan*, *choline*, and *phenylalanine*. All of these chemicals enhance the neurotransmitters associated with memory. Before studying, try a light, protein-rich meal of eggs, turkey, and fish. All of these foods release the memory enhancing chemicals. The better the connections, the more you comprehend.

Likewise, before you take a test, stick to a light snack of energy boosting and relaxing foods. A glass of milk, a piece of fruit, or some peanuts all release various memory-boosting chemicals and help you to relax and focus on the subject at hand.

2. Learn to take great notes. A by-product of our modern culture is that we have grown accustomed to getting our information in short doses (i.e. TV news sound bites or USA Today style newspaper articles.)

Consequently, we've subconsciously trained ourselves to assimilate information better in neat little packages. If your notes are scrawled all over the paper, it fragments the flow of the information. Strive for clarity. Newspapers use a standard format to achieve clarity. Your notes can be much clearer through use of proper formatting. A very effective format is called the *"Cornell Method."*

> Take a sheet of loose-leaf lined notebook paper and draw a line all the way down the paper about 1-2" from the left-hand edge.

> Draw another line across the width of the paper about 1-2" up from the bottom. Repeat this process on the reverse side of the page.

Look at the highly effective result. You have ample room for notes, a left hand margin for special emphasis items or inserting supplementary data from the textbook, a large area at the bottom for a brief summary, and a little rectangular space for just about anything you want.

LIBRARY MEDIA

3. Get the concept then the details. Too often we focus on the details and don't gather an understanding of the concept. However, if you simply memorize only dates, places, or names, you may well miss the whole point of the subject.

A key way to understand things is to put them in your own words. If you are working from a textbook, automatically summarize each paragraph in your mind. If you are outlining text, don't simply copy the author's words.

Rephrase them in your own words. You remember your own thoughts and words much better than someone else's, and subconsciously tend to associate the important details to the core concepts.

4. Ask Why? Pull apart written material paragraph by paragraph and don't forget the captions under the illustrations.

Example: If the heading is "Stream Erosion," flip it around to read "Why do streams erode?" Then answer the questions.

If you train your mind to think in a series of questions and answers, not only will you learn more, but it also helps to lessen the test anxiety because you are used to answering questions.

5. Read for reinforcement and future needs. Even if you only have 10 minutes, put your notes or a book in your hand. Your mind is similar to a computer; you have to input data in order to have it processed. *By reading, you are creating the neural connections for future retrieval.* The more times you read something, the more you reinforce the learning of ideas.

Even if you don't fully understand something on the first pass, *your mind stores much of the material for later recall.*

6. Relax to learn, and go into exile. Our bodies respond to an inner clock called biorhythms. Burning the midnight oil works well for some people, but not everyone.

If possible, set aside a particular place to study that is free of distractions. Shut off the television, cell phone, and pager and exile your friends and family during your study period.

If you really are bothered by silence, try background music. Light classical music at a low volume has been shown to aid in concentration over other types. Music that evokes pleasant emotions without lyrics is highly suggested. Try just about anything by Mozart. It relaxes you.

TEACHER CERTIFICATION STUDY GUIDE

7. Use arrows, not highlighters. At best, it's difficult to read a page full of yellow, pink, blue, and green streaks. Try staring at a neon sign for a while and you'll soon see that the horde of colors obscure the message.

A quick note, a brief dash of color, an underline, and an arrow pointing to a particular passage is much clearer than a horde of highlighted words.

8. Budget your study time. Although you shouldn't ignore any of the material, *allocate your available study time in the same ratio that topics may appear on the test.*

TEACHER CERTIFICATION STUDY GUIDE

Testing Tips:

1. Get smart, play dumb. Don't read anything into the question. Don't make an assumption that the test writer is looking for something else than what is asked. Stick to the question as written and don't read extra things into it.

2. Read the question and all the choices *twice* before answering the question. You may miss something by not carefully reading, and then re-reading both the question and the answers.

If you really don't have a clue as to the right answer, leave it blank on the first time through. Go on to the other questions, as they may provide a clue as to how to answer the skipped questions.

If later on, you still can't answer the skipped ones . . . ***Guess.*** The only penalty for guessing is that you *might* get it wrong. Only one thing is certain; if you don't put anything down, you will get it wrong!

3. Turn the question into a statement. Look at the way the questions are worded. The syntax of the question usually provides a clue. Does it seem more familiar as a statement rather than as a question? Does it sound strange?

By turning a question into a statement, you may be able to spot if an answer sounds right, and it may also trigger memories of material you have read.

4. Look for hidden clues. It's actually very difficult to compose multiple-foil (choice) questions without giving away part of the answer in the options presented.

In most multiple-choice questions you can often readily eliminate one or two of the potential answers. This leaves you with only two real possibilities and automatically your odds increase to fifty-fifty for very little work.

5. Trust your instincts. For every fact that you have read, you subconsciously retain something of that knowledge. On questions that you aren't really certain about, go with your basic instincts. **Your first impression of how to answer a question is usually correct.**

6. Mark your answers directly on the test booklet. Don't bother trying to fill in the optical scan sheet on the first pass through the test.

7. Watch the clock! You have a set amount of time to answer the questions. Don't get bogged down trying to answer a single question at the expense of 10 questions you can more readily answer.

LIBRARY MEDIA

TEACHER CERTIFICATION STUDY GUIDE

COMPETENCY 1.0 PROGRAM ADMINISTRATION

Skill 1.1 Organization, administration, and evaluation of the library media center

Resource organization systems vary from school to school, based on factors such as user demand, storage considerations, staff limitations and preferences, and processing procedures. Some media specialists separate specific age/reading level collections for ease of location, especially with younger children. Audiovisual and multi-media kits may be shelved with print material if they can be circulated to all users. Visibility creates greater use. However, collection security for instructional materials and equipment must also be considered. Organizational procedures should be logical and follow standardized procedures as much as possible.

The objective of organization systems:

1. Ready access. To make resources, regardless of format, easy to locate, a bibliographic control system must be in place. A catalog, preferably automated, should include all print and non-print resources and equipment.

2. Circulation ease. If the card catalog is not automated, the media center staff should keep accurate circulation records to facilitate retrieval and inventory. If audiovisual materials or equipment are not housed near the circulation area, a paper record is necessary. For equipment not housed in the media center itself, location information must appear in the catalog.

Until the passage of the **Elementary and Secondary Education Act in 1965**, which encouraged the evolution of school libraries into library media centers, school libraries were repositories of print material, mainly reference books and fiction. School librarians, rarely having a support staff, circulated and processed materials, supervised student behavior in the library, maintained the collection, and distributed limited equipment. The explosion of information and the retrieval systems for accessing that information has revolutionized the role of the school library media specialist (3.0) and the program she oversees (1.2). Studies in child development by Jean Piaget, Erik Erikson and Lawrence Kohlberg had begun to affect collection development in post-World War II America. Learning style theories from Abraham Maslow's hierarchy to **Bloom's Taxonomy** and Howard Gardner's eight intelligences have modified classroom teaching.

> **Learn more about ESEA:**
> http://www.ed.gov/legislation/ESEA/toc.html

> **Learn more about Bloom's Taxonomy:**
> http://en.wikipedia.org/wiki/Benjamin_Bloom

As libraries began to evolve into full service media centers and school media specialists became instructional consultants to teachers, all aspects of program development were influenced by the need to know those factors that influence children's learning. The ability to assess the needs of student users of a particular media center's services and resources becomes a collaborative effort with classroom teachers who have daily contact with their students; thus, the move to cooperative planning and cooperative learning in the 1990s.

In the 1980s legislative actions at the national and state level (1.1), government concern for widespread literacy, and document findings such as those in *A Nation at Risk* all reinforced that instruction must be improved in all areas. As a result of private publications, such as James Naisbitt's *Megatrends* and *Megatrends 2000* and research by the staff of *School Library Media Quarterly*, the issue of providing more than mere access to the wealth of information affects libraries in the public and private sector. Ultimately, the school library media specialist becomes the agent through which the most aggressive change will occur.

In 1988, *Information Power: Guidelines for School Library Media Programs* was published under the supervision of AASL president, Karen Whitney, and AECT president, Elaine Didier. In the same year *Taxonomies of the School Library Media Program* by David Loertscher, senior acquisitions editor for Libraries Unlimited, appeared. In fact, there is now a considerable body of excellent reference material on school library media. In 1998, *Information Power: Building Partnerships for Learning* was published as an update to the original *Information Power*. This book focused on the importance of information literary, as well as building collaborative partnerships with teachers. This publication also included information regarding the use and management of technology.

> **Learn more about Information Power:**
> http://www.ala.org/ala/aasl/aaslproftools/informationpower/informationpower.cfm

Technology has both created the engines of access and contributed to the volume of available information. In addition to learning the types of equipment and their functions and demonstrating their use to teachers and students, the school library media specialist must also locate or design lessons that will teach the "search and sift" techniques that help them find the appropriate information for a given need. Critical evaluation of the reading and applying the new information to previous knowledge are skills that must be accomplished.

Many school library media specialists have accepted the title without making the adaptation. They feel overloaded by the magnitude of the job description. Oftentimes, districts approach technology enhancement by putting the hardware before the program.

Merely acquiring computers, CD players, networking equipment, printers, scanners, and so on in the schools achieves nothing in regard to benefit to the learners, especially if the equipment gathers dust. Program development is often an afterthought, from necessity.

Societal changes have had profound effects on schools. Ethnic diversity, non-traditional families, poverty, and population mobility have created social and cultural difficulties that did not exist thirty years ago. Furthermore, children raised in this ever-shifting social network must be prepared with skills that will enable them to become productive, literate adults. Library media centers are charged with the responsibility of motivating interest in reading as well as promoting acquisition of skills, of providing reading that will not only inform but help children learn how to cope with and enjoy life.

Issues regarding censorship and intellectual access to information increase as the volume of all types of information sources increase. Media professionals must learn how to handle challenges to the material in and accessible from their media centers, and they must guard their patrons' right to free access. Interpreting fair use and other copyright issues requires constant monitoring of court cases and changes in the law (2.3, 2.6). The impact of all of these issues will continue to affect school library media programs.

All of these factors place an administrative role on school library media specialists. They have the responsibility of directing all of the activities linked to the library media program. They must
- work collaboratively with all staff and students to ensure effective use of information resources
- promote the mission of the school library media program
- manage staff, budget, equipment and all other resources
- constantly evaluate the effectiveness of the program for quality purposes

Evaluation of school library media programs must be a continuous process. According to *Information Power: Building Partnerships for Learning,* the goals for the school library media specialist when conducting assessments are:
- stay abreast of current trends in evaluation
- work collaboratively with staff and administrators to determine if curricular needs are being met
- schedule regular intervals for data collection
- use qualitative and quantitative data
- make program decisions based upon the assessment findings
- report results regularly to staff

Skill 1.2 **Planning and evaluation: assessing needs, planning objectives, setting priorities, evaluating, defining the center's mission and philosophy, and site-based management**

Proper planning is essential to the success of any school library media program. The planning process will take determination, but a quality media program is of great benefit to any school.

For the planning process to be successful, it must have the support of your principal. Other key people within your school must be included, such as teachers, school support staff, parents, and students. This group of individuals would become part of a school library planning committee sometimes known as the **Media Advisory Committee (MAC) or Media and Technology Advisory Committee (MTAC)**. Utilizing such a committee approach is reflective of site-based management. Site-based management decisions are made by a group of stakeholders or committee rather than being left to the discretion of one person.

> Learn more about Media Advisory Committees:
> http://www.ncwiseowl.org/Impact/progAdmin.htm#mtac

One of the first things the planning committee must do is **develop a mission statement** that defines the core purpose of the school library media program. The mission statement must become the focus from which all goals are formed and decisions are made.

> Learn more about Mission Statements
> http://www.franklincovey.com/fc/library_and_resources/mission_statement_builder

The mission of any organization, business, or educational institution should evolve from the needs and expectations of its customers. In the case of the school library media center, its mission must parallel the school's mission and attend to the users' needs for resources and services.

The school library media program should examine school and student characteristics.

School characteristics:

1. The mission of the school library media center should reflect and be in harmony with the stated school mission.
2. The program's mission should reflect the curricular direction of the school: academic, vocational, or compensatory.
3. The mission should reflect the willingness of the administration and faculty to support the program.

Student characteristics:

1. The mission is influenced by pupil demographics: age, achievement and ability levels, reading levels, and learning styles.
2. The mission may indicate the students' interest in self-directed learning and exploratory reading.
3. The mission reflects support from parents and community groups.

> **Learn more about types of evaluation criteria**
> http://www.socialresearchmethods.net/kb/datatype.php

Once a mission has been defined, it is important to assess the status of the program and see how closely it follows that mission. Gathering this information is essential to the formation of effective goals and objectives.

It is important to note that evaluation is an ongoing process. It must occur prior to determining goals and objectives and on a regular basis thereafter to ensure they are being met.

A wide variety of evaluation criteria may be used. The criteria may be

1. Diagnostic. These are standards based on conditions existing in programs that have already been judged excellent.
2. Projective. These standards are guidelines for ideal conditions.
3. Quantitative. These standards require numerical measurement.
4. Qualitative. These standards are designed to express essentially the measured criteria as quantitative without exact numerical amounts.

Most school library media programs evaluations have been diagnostic or qualitative. Diagnostic prescriptions alone make no allowances for specific conditions in given schools and are often interpreted too liberally; qualitative prescriptions alone are difficult to measure or sustain. Projective standards are usually broad national guidelines that serve best as long-range goals. Preferably, a program evaluation, utilizing a combination of quantitative and qualitative standards, produces results that can lead to modified objectives.

Statistics to substantiate quantitative standards can be derived from:

1. Usage statistics from automated circulation systems. These indicate frequency of materials use.
2. Inventory figures. Resource turnover, loss and damage, and missing materials statistics indicate extent of use. Total materials count can substantiate materials per student criteria.
3. Individual circulation logs. Such logs indicate the frequency of patron use of library materials and the types of materials used.

4. Class scheduling log. Depending on the amount of data acquired when a visit is scheduled, several facts can be determined: proportion of staff and student body using materials and services; the frequency of use of specific resources or services; the age levels of users; specific subgroups being served; and subject matter preferences.

Evidence of meeting qualitative standards can be derived from
1. Lesson plans. Careful planning will reveal the frequency of use of resources and specific classroom objectives planned cooperatively with faculty. The plan should also specify the effectiveness with which the students achieved the lesson objectives.
2. Personnel evaluations. Most districts have formative and/or summative evaluations for the professional/paraprofessional/non-professional staff. Student aides should receive educational credit for their services hours. Completion of specific skills and termination grades can provide both quantitative and qualitative data.
3. Surveys. A systematic written evaluation should be conducted annually to obtain input from students, teachers, and parents on the success of program objectives.
4. Conferences/Library Advisory Committee meetings. Faculty members' and students' comments can provide qualitative assessment of the value of the materials and services provided.
5. Criterion-referenced or teacher-created tests. These assessments can be used to evaluate student effectiveness in acquiring information skills or content area skills.

The purposes of evaluation are to determine if all aspects of planning and implementation have been successfully accomplished. If evaluation shows unsuccessful outcomes, then the program must be modified. Successful outcomes can be used to confirm program objectives and to promote the media center programs.

Some strategies for the use of program evaluation include

1. To produce an annual report to be included in the school's annual report to parents or other publications for circulation in the community.
2. To review and modify long-range goals and plan immediate changes in short-range goals.
3. To lobby for budgetary or personnel support.
4. To solicit assistance from faculty and administration in making curricular or instructional changes to maximize use of media center materials, equipment, and services.
5. To plan greater involvement of students in academic and personal use of media center materials and services.

There are now so many outstanding resources, and the technology to easily identify these resources, that the task can be managed by following a few simple steps.

1. Rely on the information provided in this guide's resource list. If your school or district professional library does not contain these resources, visit the public library in the nearest large city or a university library where information sciences are taught.
2. Give your school media program a close examination before doing your research. Study any written evaluations by media personnel, school improvement committees, library advisory committees, or annual reports. Informally survey a cross-section of students and teachers to gather input about their perceptions of the materials and services that are provided.
3. Make a list of questions based on the concerns that result from your evaluation. Peruse the questions in Chapter 1 of *Information Power* to see if there are any pertinent areas that have not yet been addressed.
4. Do your research.
5. Produce a written evaluation of your school's library media program based on your findings. Submit this evaluation to the principal and plan with her the best way to communicate the information to students, teachers, and parents.
6. Gather input from all groups to whom your evaluation is presented.
7. Meet with the Library Media Advisory Committee or equivalent group to formulate program changes. Be sure to include students and parents or lay community members on this committee.
8. Implement the changes and plan subsequent evaluations.

Once an initial program evaluation has been completed, program goals and objectives may be determined. These goals and objectives help to break down the overall vision into areas that the school feels are most important for the successful operation of a school library media program. Some of these goals may already be determined by national or state guidelines that districts administrators have agreed to maintain. Sometimes, a district operates without a program to guide school library media centers. In that case, each school must be responsible not only for setting its own criteria but also for inspiring some district planning.

The first step would be to define major goals. A goal is a broad statement of an intended outcome that reflects the mission of the school library media program that provides direction.

Learn more about creating long-range plans
http://www.libraryhq.com/plans.html

A **goal is a long-range plan**. Therefore, when planning a school library media program based on an assessment of school and student characteristics, the program planning team should factor in these elements.

A long-range plan should

1. Extend from 3 to 5 years.
2. Incorporate the goals of the other departments (grade levels or content teams) in the school.
3. Be stated in terms that are non-limiting. The goal should be an achievable aim, not a pipe dream.

Specific goals for school library media centers are outlined in *Information Power: Building Partnerships for Learning*. Key points include:

- providing access to resources and information through integrated activities on a variety of levels
- providing physical access to a wide variety of resources and information from various locations including outside agencies and electronic resources
- assisting patrons in locating and evaluating information
- collaborating with teachers and others
- facilitating the lifelong learning process
- building a school library media program that acts as the hub of all learning within the school
- providing resources that embrace differences culturally and socially and support concepts of intellectual freedom

After the major goals have been defined, objectives must be determined. An objective is a specific statement of a measurable result that will occur by a particular time, i.e. it must specify the conditions and criteria to be met effectively. Objectives reflect short-term priorities. Objectives have a specific format. They must contain an action verb and must be measurable. A few of the action verbs often seen in objectives are as follows: discuss, define, compare, identify, explain, and design.

An objective is a short-range plan. A short-range plan should be one part of a longer range plan that is

1. Accomplishable in one year or less.
2. Linked meaningfully in a logical progression to the expressed goal.
3. Flexible, as most objectives must be processed through affected groups before finalization.

In an Olympic year an appropriate example of goals and objectives might be

Goal: To win an Olympic medal.
Objectives:

1. To increase my speed by 0.05 seconds per meter by June 30.
2. To double my practice time during the two weeks before the competition begins.
3. To lose 3 pounds before my weigh-in.

If translated into goals and objectives for library media centers it may read as follows:

Goal: To develop a collection more suited to the academic demands of the curriculum
Objectives:

1. To increase non-fiction collection by 10% in the next school year.
2. To ensure readability levels suited to gifted students for 5% of new selections.

Goal: To provide telecommunications services within three years.
Objectives:

1. To design a model for instructional use in 2005
2. To plan for equipment and facilities needs in 2006
3. To implement the model with a control group in 2007

If a school seeks or wishes to maintain accreditation with the regional Association of Colleges and Schools using that organization's recommendations is an excellent way to set program goals and objectives. Because the Association of Colleges and Schools requires every accredited school to conduct an intensive ten-year reevaluation and five-year interim reviews, the library media center program planners may wish to coordinate their own study with the reviews of this regional agency.

Skill 1.3 Management: budgeting, staffing, training, and supervising student aides and volunteers

In preparation for **constructing the budget** for the school library media center, the school media professionals need to consider

1. The standards set by state departments of education, local school boards, and regional accreditation associations. Changes in standards sometimes necessitate changes in local budget planning.
2. The sources of funds that support the media center program.
3. The prioritized list of program goals and the cost of meeting these goals.

> **Learn more about developing a media budget:**
>
> http://www.ala.org/Template.cfm?Section=budgeting

Determining the relationship between program goals and funding involve the study of

1. Past inventories and projections of future needs.
2. Quantitative and qualitative collection standards at all levels.
3. School and district curriculum plans.
4. Community needs.
5. Fiscal deadlines.

AASL/AECT provides guidelines for four factors in calculating the budget for the print and non-print collection: variation in student population, attrition by weeding, attrition by date, and attrition by loss. A formula for an estimated budget is then calculated based on points established for each of these factors. The estimation for replacement is figured on a base number of collection items required regardless of school size. The minimum collection standard is determined by the state or regional accreditation requirements.

> **Learn more about AASL**
>
> http://www.ala.org/ala/aasl/aaslindex.cfm

Another method of estimating a budget for the print collection is based on the types of materials needed: replacement books, periodicals, books for growth and expansion, and reference books. It is recommended that 5% of the total books in the print collection be used in the formula.

> **Learn more about AECT**
>
> http://www.aect.org/default.asp

Thus, the formula is
5% × number of books × average cost of book = replacement cost.

For periodicals, multiply the number of periodicals by the average subscription price.

Use the following figures to calculate book collection expansion: at 90% fulfillment of basic requirement, add 3%-5%; at 75%-90% fulfillment, use 10%-15%; and at less than 75%, use 15%-25%. For reference books, multiply the number of sets times the average set price.

In a hypothetical school of 1000-1500 students, accrediting agencies recommend a base collection of 10 volumes per student, i.e. a minimum collection of 10,000 books for a population of 1000 students. If that school has only 75% (7650 or fewer), the expansion formula should be

$$15\text{-}25\% \times \text{existing collection} \times \text{average book price}.$$

If our hypothetical school has 7500 books, the formula might be

$$20\% \times 7500 \times \$20 = \$30,000.$$

If the school has 75-90% of the recommended 10,200 books, we can meet expansion guidelines by adding 10-15% of the collection.

The formula would then be

$$10\% \times 8160 \times \$20 = \$16,320.$$

Finally, if the school is at 90-100% of the recommendation, we expand by 3-5% or

$$5\% \times 9690 \times \$20 = \$9690.$$

The accreditation standard for periodicals is no fewer than 10 titles or one for each 25 students—whichever is greater. After the print subscriptions equal 30, the remaining requirement may be satisfied with non-print resources. Let's assume that this school has 50 print subscriptions and 2 non-print databases. If the average print subscription price is $20 annually and the average non-print database is $2000, this school should estimate $5000 for periodicals.

If two sets of reference books at an average price of $1000 are needed, the estimated cost is $2000.

Calculations for audiovisual materials follow the same basic pattern. For our school, let's assume that we have calculated this figure into our print collection estimate.

Equipment estimations are based on multiplying four elements: the current inventory replacement value; replacement of lost, stolen, or damaged items; average age of the equipment; and the inflation rate. If our hypothetical school has a current value of $200,000, the average age of items is 5 years, the average replacement cost is $200, and the inflation rate is 1.3 percent, the equipment estimation would be calculated as follows:

$$\$200{,}000 \times 5 = \$1{,}000{,}000 \times .013 = 13{,}000 + \$200 = \$13{,}200$$

The total estimated collection budget then equals the sum of estimates. At 90% satisfaction of collection requirement, our total would be

$$\$9690 + \$5000 + \$2000 + \$13{,}200 = \$29{,}890$$

In districts in which the school library media center allocation is not calculated on local recommendations but on an across-the-board per capita figure, the school library media specialist must then work with the administration to secure necessary funds from the school budget. If funds are not categorized at the district level, the school library media specialist must then set a percentage for each category based on the previously discussed factors.

Having considered all factors, the budget process should parallel budget plans to the program goals and objectives. To achieve this correlation the process should follow these steps.

1. Communicate program and budget considerations to administration, faculty, students, and community groups, allowing sufficient time for input from all groups.
2. Work with representatives from all groups to finalize short-range objectives and review long-range goals for use of funds.
3. Build a system of flexible encumbrance and transferal of funds as changes in needs occur.
4. As part of the program promotion, communicate budgetary concerns to all interested parties.

Unlike public libraries, school library media centers are not usually the recipients of endowments or private gifts. School library media centers receive money from local and state tax dollars. The major portion of the funds comes from district allotments for instructional materials or capital outlay that are regulated by the state. Schools that have accreditation must adhere to regional guidelines that assure that accreditation. The funding formulas specifically used for school library media budgets vary from district to district but basically comply with the following regulations.

Local:
Schools often receive funding from the area's governing officials that can be applied to school library programs. At the school level, many school libraries host book fairs to supplement funding received from other sources.

State:

1. Local operation. School library media centers funds are generally allocated from the district operating budget. The funds may be administered at the district or school level according to a per capita figure, adequate to meet operation costs and contractual obligations.
2. Regional guidelines. Each regional accrediting agency produces an expenditures requirement based on student body size, allowing a school to average expenditures over a three-year period in which averaged expenditures do not fall below the standard.
3. State funds provided by special legislation. Most special funds have been in the form of block grants. Block grants are funds earmarked for a specific purpose. Schools generally must apply for such funds. One example is the technology block grants that have appeared in recent years. These grants have provided funds for retrofitting schools to create local area networks, wide-area networks, and telecommunications services.

Federal:

1. Block grants included in federal education acts (4.6.3). Awarded to states or specific districts, these grants are limited in scope and time. They must be applied for on a competitive basis and renewal depends on the recipient's ability to prove that grant objectives have been met.

2. Current federal funds are earmarked for innovative technologies, not operating costs.

In addition to official funding sources, there are other forms of assistance from the community that should be reflected in the budget plan. Because this assistance is in the form of service rather than real dollars, estimated values must be determined. Some community assistance includes

1. Partnerships with local businesses. Free wiring from cable television companies, guest speakers, distance learning opportunities, and workshops in new technologies are just a few possible services.
2. Education support groups. The education committee of the local chamber of commerce, a private education economic council, or parent associations may conduct fund-raisers or offer mini-grants.
3. Corporate grants. Many large companies provide grants for specific topics such as technology, science, math and reading. The grant may involve providing equipment or funds to be used for a specific purpose.

The American Association of School Librarians (AASL) recommends that a school library media center by a licensed school library media specialist with a Master's degree from an **American Library Association (ALA)** or National Council for the Accreditation of Teacher Education (NCATE) accredited educational program and qualified support staff.

> **Learn more about the American Library Association:**
>
> http://www.ala.org

Professional responsibilities and activities are those outlined in the performance indicators throughout Competency 4. The school library media specialist has responsibility for developing program goals, collection development, budget management, consultation with teachers in using existing resources or producing new materials, provision for student instruction and staff development, and overseeing the paraprofessional and nonprofessional staffs.

The paraprofessional is a person qualified for a special area of media such as graphics, photography, instructional television, electronics, media production, or computer technology. Often called a media or technical assistant, this person has training in his specialty and some education training but does not have a bachelor's degree in library or information sciences. The media or technical assistant may have an AA or BA/BS degree in his/her specialty. Some community colleges offer certificates in Library Assistantship.

The paraprofessional's responsibilities are in the areas of production, maintenance, and special services to students and teachers. Some of the duties might include

1. Working with teachers in the design and production of media for classroom instruction.
2. Creating promotional materials and preparing special need media (video yearbook, audio or videotape duplication, preparation of materials for faculty meetings and staff development activities).
3. Operating and maintaining production equipment (laminator, audio and video devices).
4. Maintaining computers and peripherals.
5. Evaluating media and equipment collection and recommending purchases.
6. Developing ways to use existing and emerging technologies.
7. Assisting teachers and students in locating and using media and equipment.
8. Repairing or making provisions for repair of materials and equipment.
9. Circulating equipment.
10. Maintaining records on circulation, maintenance, and repair of media and equipment.

The non-professional staff assumes responsibility for operational procedures (clerical, secretarial, technical, maintenance) that relieve the school library professional and paraprofessional of routine tasks so they can better perform their responsibilities.

Some specific nonprofessional activities:

1. Conducting accounting and bookkeeping procedures.
2. Unpacking, processing and shelving new materials.
3. Processing correspondence, records, manuals, and the like.
4. Circulating materials and equipment.
5. Assisting with materials production.
6. Assisting with maintenance and repair of materials and equipment.
7. Handling accounting procedures.
8. Assisting with inventory.
9. Assisting with services provided by electronic and computer equipment.

The diversity of user needs, school enrollments, and school/district support services are some factors that affect staff size. Some of the duties of different levels of staff persons overlap and differ only in the amount of decision-making and accountability.

If the school places a high priority on an efficient library media center program, there should be a minimum of two full-time professionals, one paraprofessional and two nonprofessionals, one to function as an office manager and one as a technical assistant.

However, ALA and **NEA** standards for School Media Programs recommended two support staff for each specialist in any school with under 2000 enrollment. Accrediting standards recommend that in a school with two specialists on staff, two paraprofessionals may be hired in lieu of an additional professional. Unfortunately, when schools are looking to save money, it is generally the support staff who are cut.

> **Learn more about NEA**
>
> http://www.nea.org/index.html

TEACHER CERTIFICATION STUDY GUIDE

When the support staff is reduced, the professional must assume operational duties that detract from his professional responsibilities. Volunteers can help with circulation and supplemental tasks that reflect their unique talents and experiences, but they should never be used as substitutes for paid clerical and technical staff. Student assistants, like volunteers, may be trained to assist the media specialist but should not be given duties that are the responsibilities of paid nonprofessionals. They might assist with production of materials, maintenance of the decoration and physical appearance of the center, instruction in materials location, use of electronic/computer databases, use or maintenance of equipment, and shelving books and periodicals. It is recommended that student aides be given course credit or certificates of achievement to reward them for their services.

Most untrained support staff will need to be trained on the job.

1. Using the district's job description and evaluation instrument for the particular position, prioritize the skills in order from greatest to least immediacy.
2. Determine the already mastered skills by observing performance.
3. Plan a systematic training of remaining skills to be addressed one at a time.

Supervision of media professionals is the responsibility of an administrator. Supervision of support staff is the responsibility of the head library media specialist (if that position is administrative) or of an administrator with input from the media specialist. Periodic oral evaluations and annual written evaluations using an appropriate instrument should be conducted for each media staff member. These evaluations should result in suggestions for training or personal development.

Skill 1.4 Establishing policies and procedures

In addition to the AASL/AECT guidelines (1.7) also endorsed by the NEA, guidelines are available from state departments of education.

> **Learn more about policies and procedures**
>
> http://www.ala.org/ala/oif/statementspols/statementspolicies.htm

The following summarizes AASL/AECT guidelines. The role of the school library media specialist is three-fold. The information specialist meets program needs by providing

1. Access to the facility and materials that is non-restrictive—economically, ethnically, and physically.
2. Communication to teachers, students, administrators, and parents concerning new materials, services, and technologies.
3. Efficient retrieval and information sharing systems.

LIBRARY MEDIA 17

The teacher specialist is charged with the responsibilities of

1. Integrating information skills into the content curriculum.
2. Providing access to and instruction in the use of technology.
3. Planning jointly with classroom teachers the use and production of media appropriate to learner needs.
4. Using various instructional methods to provide staff development in policies, procedures, media production, and technology use.

The instructional consultant uses her expertise to

1. Participate in curriculum development and assessment.
2. Assist teachers in acquiring information skills that they can incorporate into classroom instruction.
3. Design a scope and sequence of teaching information skills.
4. Provide leadership in the use and assessment of information technologies.

The issue of flexible access is especially distressing to elementary school library media specialists who are placed in the "related arts" wheel, providing planning time for art, music, and physical education teachers. "Closed" or rigid scheduling, i.e. scheduling classes to meet regularly for instruction in the library, prohibits the implementation of the integrated program philosophy essential to the principles of intellectual freedom.

The **AASL Position Statement on Flexible Scheduling** asserts that schools must adopt a philosophy of full integration of library media into the total educational program. This integration assures a partnership of students, teachers, and school library media specialists in the use of readily accessible materials and services when they are appropriate to the classroom curriculum

Learn more about flexible scheduling
http://www.ala.org/ala/aasl/aaslproftools/resourceguides/flexiblescheduling.cfm

All parties in the school community—teachers, principal, district administration, and school board—must share the responsibility for contributing to flexible access.

Research on the validity of flexible access reinforces the need for cooperative planning with teachers, an objective that cannot be met if the school library media specialist has no time for the required planning sessions. Rigid scheduling denies students the freedom to come to the library during the school day for pleasurable reading and self-motivated inquiry activities vital to the development of critical thinking, problem solving, and exploratory skills. Without flexible access, the library becomes just another self-contained classroom.

A policy is the written statement of principle in which the policy-making agency guarantees a management practice or course of action that is expedient and consistent. A procedure is the course of action taken to execute the policy. In government, legislation is policy and law enforcement is procedure.

Educational policy makers include the Congress and state legislatures, state and local school boards, national library media organizations, and school library media program managers. Policies adopted at the local level must support district school board policies and state laws.

Regulations concerning certification, state budget allocations, and standards for selecting and approving state-adopted instructional materials are developed at the state level.

Matters such as collection development and responding to challenges of materials are usually set at the district level.

Local issues such as hours of operation, circulation of materials and equipment, and personnel supervision are set by the appropriate school policy makers for library media.

Procedures for administering district and state policies are usually determined by usual practice or local precedence.

Procedures for specific administration tasks such as determining budget categories, expending funds, maintaining collection size and so many others should be clearly stated in a school library media procedures manual.

There are two basic sources for district policies: school board rules and the procedures manual from district media services offices. Information provided in these documents should be reviewed before any school level planning is done.

It is also necessary to know which policies and procedures are the responsibility of the district and which ones are the responsibility of the school. For example, school boards are charged with the responsibility to set propriety standards for instructional material selection (1.1). However, school boards do not select the texts or library books for individual schools. Procedures for implementing propriety standards are determined at each school site based on the needs of its students.

School boards may set policy for a challenge and identify a procedure for its sequential investigation. The school library media specialist as a defender of intellectual freedom and a trained educator should have the latitude to recommend and purchase quality materials. She should also be prepared to substantiate those purchases in terms of readability, social appropriateness, and artistic quality.

School districts are bound by law to maintain a properly certified staff, but it is the obligation of the employee to learn what and where professional development activities are available, to take a specified number of course credits within a given time period, and to submit proof of same to the certification officer prior to the deadline in the renewal year.

Operational procedures change from district-to-district. Some counties have centralized reprographics facilities; therefore, district policies are set for reproduction of materials that comply with copyright laws and district procedures for formatting, according to the type of equipment used, are spelled out in a printed manual that should be available at all school sites.

Some counties have centralized materials processing so that classification and cataloging procedures are administered at the county level.

Participants	Role
Administrator	clarifies school vision and goals.
Media specialist	identifies factors such as time, personnel, resources, and budget that affect school goals.
Teacher	identifies media center resources and services that correlate with instruction.
Student	identifies materials and activities that fulfill learning needs.
Parents (Optional)	identify avenues of communication with parents and community.

Once the advisory committee has formulated acceptable policies and procedures, the district director and/or directors of elementary and secondary instruction should review and provide input before adoption.

The most efficient method of communicating policies and procedures to the faculty is the library media procedures manual. This manual should first present the mission and long-range objectives and then the specific policies designed to meet these objectives. Specific procedures for using the resources and services should include scheduling of the facility, circulation of materials and equipment, requests for consultation or instruction, and requests for production of media.

Communicating policies to students is best facilitated by a structured orientation program and frequent visits to the media center to practice applying those procedures. In schools with closed circuit television, a live or taped program concerning library media use can be very successful.

Skill 1.5 Renovating facilities and planning new facilities: technology planning, educational specifications, and access for the disabled

Planning for renovation or new **facilities** needs to be a team effort that would include a school level planning committee, district level representatives, planning consultants, the architect and builders.

> **Learn more about planning and renovating library facilities**
>
> http://www.ala.org/Template.cfm?Section=equipment

The school level planning committee should include the school library media specialist, technology specialist, principal, teachers, students, parents, school board member, system-level media director, system level technology director, and superintendent. The responsibilities of this group would be to assist with the planning process, determine education specifications, determine technology needs, select furniture, and set priorities or the essentials needed to ensure the success of the school library media program.

There are important design elements to consider when renovating or building new facilities.

1. Traffic flow should provide easy, logical access to all spaces.
2. A realistic assessment of security needs will provide for material detection systems, alarms or locks to protect electronic equipment, and convenient placement of communications devices.
3. Proper placement of electrical outlets, fire extinguishers, smoke detectors, and thermostats ensures safety for users and convenience for the staff.
4. Provision must be made for the physically impaired to have barrier-free access to the center and its resources.
5. All areas requiring supervision should be readily visible from other areas of the center.
6. There should be a carefully planned relationship of spaces used for supporting activities and services.

The specifics of spatial arrangement depend upon the types and quantities of resources and services provided. New school design should place the media center in a central location, easily accessible to all academic areas. Within the center itself, the following spatial arrangement factors should be addressed.

1. A large central area for reading, listening, viewing, and computing, that has ready access to materials and equipment. AASL/AECT guidelines recommend that this main seating area be 25%-75% of the total square footage allocation, depending on program requirements. 40 square feet should be allotted per student user. Within this area or peripheral to it should be smaller areas that provide for independent study or accommodate students with physical impairments. Seating should be adequate to accommodate the number of users during peak hours.

Accrediting guidelines recommend floor space and seating to accommodate 10% of the student body, but the media center should not be expected to seat fewer than 40 or more than 100 students at one time.

2. Areas for small or medium-sized group activities. These areas may be acoustically special spaces adjacent to the central seating area or conference rooms, computer labs, or storytelling space. AASL/AECT recommends 1-3 areas or approximately 150 square feet with ample electrical outlets, good lighting and acoustics, and a wall screen.

3. Space to house and display the collection. Materials that can be circulated outside the center should be easily accessible from the main seating area. Index tools should be highly visible and in the immediate proximity to the collections they index. A supervised circulation desk with easy access to non-circulating databases (periodicals, CD-ROM disks, microform, and videotape collections) should be close to the center's main entrance. AASL/AECT recommends 400 square feet minimum for stacks with an additional 200 foot allowance per 500 additional students.

4. A reference materials area within or adjacent to the central seating area. The recommended area allowance is part of the total allotted for the stacks.

5. Space for a professional collection and work area where the faculty and media professionals can work privately. This area should be approximately 1 square foot per student.

6. Administrative offices, with areas for resource and equipment processing, materials duplication, and business materials storage. An area no smaller than 200 square feet should be available for offices alone and double that area if in-house processing is done.

7. Equipment storage and circulation area close to administrative offices and with access to outside corridor. Space for maintenance and repair is optional depending on available staff to attend to these duties. This space should be no less than 400 square feet for storage with another 150 square feet if repair facilities are necessary.

8. A media production area with space and equipment for production of audio and videotaping, graphics design, photography, computer programming, and photocopying. (In some secondary schools, a dark room is included. Other schools with commercial photography classes and a full photography lab may seek services through the photography teacher.) This area may be as small as 50 square feet or as large as 700 square feet in a school with 500 students depending on the amount of equipment required to suit media production needs; in a school with 1000 or more students, at least 700-900 square feet should be allotted for media production.

9. A television production studio for formal TV production class instruction and preparing special programming. Space for distribution of closed circuit programs and satellite transmissions should also be provided. A 1600 square foot studio (preferably 40' x 40' x 15') should be available whenever television classes are taught or studio videotaping is a program priority. AASL/AECT guidelines allow alternatives: studio space available at the district for the use of students or mini-studios/portable videotape units where videotaping is done on a small scale.
10. Recommended, but optional in many schools, is a large multi-purpose room adjacent to the media center for use as a lecture hall or meeting room. AASL/AECT recommends that this room be 700-900 square feet in a school with 500 students (i.e. classroom size) or 900-1200 square feet in a school with 1000 students. This room should be equipped for making all types of media presentations.
11. A network/server head-end area that would house network services, telephone equipment, and video distribution equipment for the entire building. The space should be from 450 to 800 square feet. Equipment for this room may include network server, routers switches, telephone patch panel, cabling, and wireless devices.
12. Network access and power outlets should be available throughout the entire media center to accommodate circulation search stations, student work stations, and other electronic devices.

Because of the diversity of services provided in a modern school library media center, it is important to foster a user-friendly atmosphere, one in which the patron is not only welcomed as a user of resources but is also involved as a producer of ideas and materials.

All facilities must follow provide access to those with physical handicaps. A few of the recommendations are:
1. Work surfaces at least 30" from the floor.
2. Clear aisle width for wheelchair access.
3. Large, clearly visible signs that include accommodations for the visually impaired.
4. Provide devices for the visually and hearing impaired. One such device is the Kurzweil-NFB (National Federation of the Blind) Reader for the visually impaired. This device reads aloud scanned or electronic text.

The library media program, in considering the academic and personal needs of the user, should provide an atmosphere in which users can attain both basic skills and enrichment goals.

Factors that influence the atmosphere:

1. Proximity to academic classes.
2. Aesthetic appearance.
3. Acoustical ceilings and floor coverings.
4. Adequate temperature control.
5. Adequate, non-glare lighting with controls for different types of viewing activities.
6. Comfortable, appropriately sized, and durable furnishings.
7. Diverse, plentiful, and current resources that are attractive to handle as well as easy to use.
8. Courteous, helpful personnel, using supervisory techniques that encourage self-exploration and creativity while protecting the rules of library etiquette.

COMPETENCY 2.0 COLLECTION DEVELOPMENT

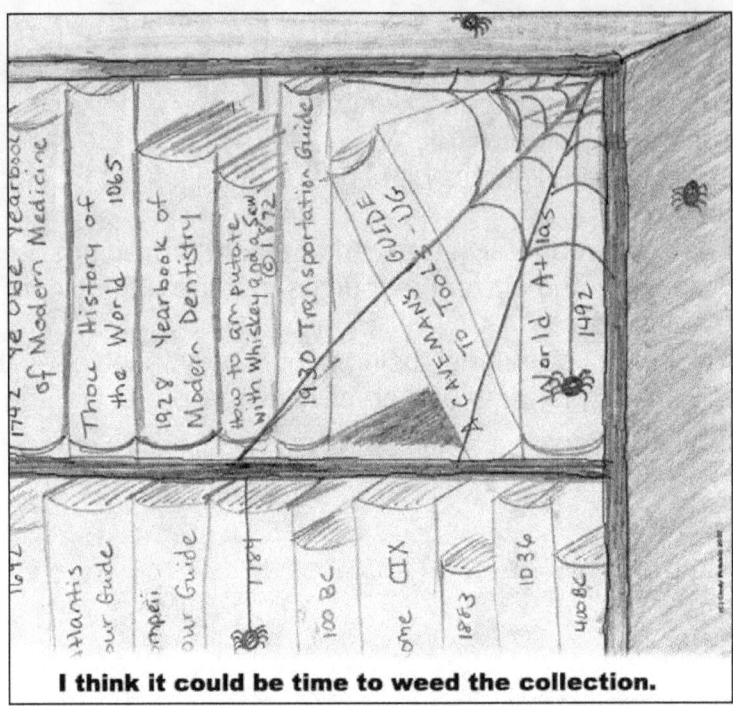

I think it could be time to weed the collection.

Skill 2.1 Selection policy: reconsideration policy, criteria for selection, collection evaluation techniques such as collection mapping and weeding

Each school library media center should develop a policy tailored to the philosophy and objectives of that school's educational program. This policy provides guidelines by which all participants in the selection process can get insight into their responsibilities. The policy statement should reflect the following factors.

> **Learn more about selection policies**
>
> http://www.ala.org/Template.cfm?Section=dealing&Template=/ContentManagement/ContentDisplay.cfm&ContentID=164386

1. Compatibility with district, state, regional, and national guidelines (1.2).
2. Adherence to the principles of intellectual freedom and the specifics of copyright law.
3. Recognition of the rights of individuals or groups to challenge policies, procedures, or selected items and the establishment of procedures for dealing fairly with such challenges.
4. Recognition of users needs and interests, including community demographics.

The policy should include the school library media center's mission and the criteria used in the selection process. General criteria for the selection of all media include

1. Authenticity. Media should be accurate, current, and authoritative. Copyright or printing dates are indicators of currency, but examination of content is often necessary to determine the relevance of the subject matter to its intended use. Research into the reputations of contributors and comparison to other materials by the same producer will provide insight into its literary quality.
2. Subject matter appropriateness. Suitability to the school's educational objectives, scope of coverage, treatment and arrangement of content, importance of content to the user, and appropriateness to users' ability levels and learning styles must be considered.
3. Appeal. Consideration of the artistic quality and language appropriateness will help in the selection of media that students will enjoy using. Properly selected materials should stimulate creativity and inspire further learning.

> **Learn more about collection development plans**
>
> http://www.ala.org/ala/alalibrary/libraryfactsheet/fact15.cfm

Elements of a **collection development plan**:

1. Knowledge of the existing collection or the ability to create a new collection.
2. Knowledge of the external environment (the school and community).
3. Assessment of school programs and user needs.
4. Development of overall policies and procedures.
5. Guidelines for specific selection decisions.
6. Evaluation criteria.
7. Establishment of a process for planning and implementing the collection plan.
8. Establishment of acquisition policies and procedures.
9. Establishment of maintenance program.
10. Establishment of procedures for evaluating the collection.

TEACHER CERTIFICATION STUDY GUIDE

Procedures for implementing the plan

1. Learn the collection. A library media specialist new to a school with an existing collection should use several approaches to becoming familiar with the collection.
    a. Browse the shelves. Note your degree of familiarity with titles. Examine items that are unfamiliar to you. Determine the relationship between the materials on similar subjects in different formats. Include the reference and professional collections in your browse. Consider the accessibility of various media and the ease with which they can be located by users.
    b. Locate the center's procedures manual. Determine explanations for any seeming irregularities in the collection.
    c. Determine if any portions of the collection are housed in areas outside the media center.

    If the library media specialist is required to create a new collection, she should
    a. Consult with the district director about new school collection policies.
    b. Examine the collections of other comparable schools.
    c. Examine companies, like Baker and Taylor's, who establish new collections based on criteria provided by the school.

2. Learn about the community.
    a. Examine the relationship of the media center to the total school program and other information agencies.
    b. Become familiar with the school, cultural, economic and political characteristics of the community and their influence on the schools.

3. Study the school's curriculum and the needs of the users (students and faculty). Examine the proportions of basic skills to enrichment offerings, academic or vocational courses, and requirements and electives. Determine the ability levels and grouping techniques for learners. Determine instructional objectives of teachers in various content areas or grade levels.

4. Examine existing policies and procedures for correlation to data acquired in researching the school and community.

5. Examine specific selection procedures to determine if guidelines are best met.

6. Examine evaluation criteria for effectiveness in maintaining an appropriate collection.

LIBRARY MEDIA

7. Examine the process to determine that accurate procedures are in place to meet the criteria.

8. Examine the acquisition plan. Determine the procedure by which materials are ordered, received, paid for and processed.
9. Examine maintenance procedures for repairing or replacing materials and equipment, replacing consumables, and discarding non-repairable items.

10. Examine the policies and procedures for evaluation, and then examine the collection itself to determine if policies and procedures are contributing to quality and quantity.

Procedures for maintaining the collection are perhaps the most important in the collection plan. The plan itself must provide efficient, economical procedures for keeping materials and equipment in usable condition.

Maintenance policies for equipment and some policies for materials are determined at the district level. Procedures to satisfy these policies are followed at the building level.

1. Replacement or discard of damaged items based on comparison of repair to replacement cost. Districts usually maintain repair contracts with external contractors for major repairs that cannot be done at the school or district media service center.
2. Equipment inventory and records on repair or disposal. Usage records help with the transfer of usable items from school to school.
3. Book bindery contracts.

Policies and procedures for periodic inspection, preventive maintenance and cleaning, and minor repairs are established and conducted at the school media center.

1. Print material. Spine and jacket repairs, taping torn pages, and replacing processing features.
2. Non-print materials. Cleaning, splicing, repairing cases.
3. Equipment. Cleaning, bulb replacement.
4. Inventory and weeding of print and non-print materials; regular replacement of worn or outdated equipment.
5. Record-keeping on items that have been lost or stolen, damaged by nature or neglect, or transferred/discarded.
6. Security systems operation, procedures for emergency disasters, and safe storage of duplicate records.

District collection development policies may be general or specific but always address areas of concern to all schools. The policy statement should reflect the philosophy of the district, and indicate the legal responsibility of the school board and the delegation of authority to specific individuals at the district and school level. One statement will usually address all instructional materials, including textbook and library media resources.

These objectives might be included in the policy:

1. To provide resources that contain information that supports and enhances the school curriculum.
2. To provide resources that satisfy user needs, abilities, and learning styles.
3. To provide resources that develop literary appreciation and artistic values.
4. To provide resources that reflect the culture and ethnic diversity of society and the contributions of members of various groups to our country's heritage.
5. To provide materials that enable students to solve problems and make judgments relevant to real life.
6. To provide resources that present opposing views on historical or contemporary issues so that students may learn to think critically and objectively.

District plans may deal with

1. Funding policies.
    a. Allocation. School media centers generally receive a portion of the general operating budget. The total amount is determined by a per student dollar amount and may come directly from the district media accounts or, under school-based management, may be apportioned from school budget categories.
    b. Authorization for purchases. These policies vary depending on who has control of the budget: principal, district or media supervisor, district purchasing agent or any combination of the three. In some districts, purchase requests must also be approved by curriculum supervisors.
    c. Supplemental sources. Federal or state block grants, endowments, or district capital outlay funds are allocated on a per capita or special project allotment basis. Responsibility for preparation of grant applications is supervised or conducted at the district level. Some districts also set policy concerning the suitability of private donations of material or property items.
2. Preview of considered materials. Some districts seek total control of previewing.

3. Collection size. Districts will frequently set minimum materials and equipment levels, especially if they aim to meet accreditation standards. These standards specify a minimum book collection of approximately 10 volumes per student. Responsibility for start-up collections at new schools are governed by district media.
4. Resource sharing. Some decisions in regards to delivery systems, cooperative funding, software licensing and liability are district determined.
5. Time constraints. All districts require that funds be expended by a specific deadline.
6. District media library policies and procedures. Materials that are either too expensive for school budgets and will be used by more than one school are maintained at the district library.
7. Equipment and materials maintenance and repair policy. Districts maintain repair contracts and set procedures for their use. Annual inventories, especially of equipment, are required and periodic assessments of policies are conducted.
8. Central processing. Available in some districts, this department processes materials for convenience and uniformity.

From time to time libraries will receive challenges regarding the content of library resources. It is important for schools to have a reconsideration policy for challenged books. According the American Library Association's (ALA) *Library Bill of Rights*, libraries are sources of information that should cover all points of view on all topics following the rules of The First Amendment. The association does not believe that information should be removed from the library for any reason if it fit the criteria of the selection policy.

> **Learn more about the *Library Bill of Rights***
>
> http://www.ala.org/ala/oif/statementspols/statementsif/librarybillrights.htm

Many school districts have a reconsideration policy in place. If a district does not, a good place to go for assistance is the ALA website. Here are a few things to consider.

1. Develop a principles statement for your library that expresses the school's position regarding access to information. *The Library Bill of Rights* will be a good reference for wording such a statement.
2. Outline a procedure for handling the challenged material. This could include notifying the principal when a challenge arises, following procedures if the complaint cannot be resolved informally, developing forms to file for formal complaints, articulating library advisory committee responsibilities, and notifying the person filing the complaint of the reconsideration committee's decision.
3. It is important to lay out the responsibilities of the school level reconsideration committee so that they will understand the procedures for handling the complaint.

It is important to make sure the resources in the school library's collection is current and meets the needs of the students. One way to accomplish this is by mapping the collection.

Collection mapping is the practice of examining the quantity and quality of your resource collection. A collection map will provide a graphic display of the extent of the collection. In other words, the collection map offers a quick snapshot of the collection.

> **Learn more about collection mapping**
>
> http://www.lmcsource.com/pdfs/CollectionMapping.pdf

The resource collection should be divided into three areas:

1. There should be a base or core collection that provides something for everyone.
2. There should be general emphasis collections that cover curricular needs for specific subjects and/or grade levels.
3. There should be specific emphasis collections that are used to cover the needs of particular units or topics.

Collection maps have many benefits. These include:

- identifying strengths and weaknesses within the collection
- evaluating whether resources match curriculum taught or state standards
- planning for purchases
- identifying sections in need of weeding
- demonstrating areas of need and areas of excellence

School libraries are sources of information for staff and students, therefore it is important that the information is current and of relevance. Most schools have a selection policy, but it is also important to have a weeding policy. Weeding the collection requires the school library media specialist to remove outdated information or worn books from the shelves.

Many resources provide assistance with weeding procedures. A few things to take into consideration when reviewing your collection for weeding are:

1. Weeding should be an ongoing process.
2. Review books for age, frequency of use, condition, multiple copies, and accuracy of information
3. Here are the suggested weeding procedures for each **Dewey** level:
   - 000 — encyclopedias every five years, other materials no more than eight years
   - 100 — five to eight years
   - 200 — can be high turnover with religious books–keep current
   - 300 — almanacs replace every two years, keep political information current
   - 400 — check for wear and tear frequently
   - 500 — continuously update to make sure scientific information is current
   - 600 — continuously update medical information as older information can be misleading or dangerous
   - 700 — keep until worn
   - 800 — keep until worn
   - 900 — weed about every two years
   - Biography — keep most current or best written titles
   - Adult fiction — weed for multiple copies, keep those in best shape and that have the most literary value
   - Young-adult and children's fiction — same as adult fiction
   - Reference — weed for currency and accuracy

> **Learn more about Dewey Classification levels**
>
> http://en.wikipedia.org/wiki/List_of_Dewey_Decimal_classes

Skill 2.2 Selecting resources: knowledge of information resources, both book and non-book; knowledge of bibliographic resources in all formats

When selecting resources for a school library, it is important to work in collaboration with teachers and follow district and state selection policies. Finding the resources can be a daunting task because there are many sources of information.

The best places to begin are review publications such as:
- *School Library Journal*
- *Booklist*
- *The Horn Book*
- *Wilson Book Review*

Each of these provides concise reviews on current books. *The Horn Book* is a collective guide that will list the ratings from the other sources listed.

Other places to locate resources include:

1. Companies who offer collection lists designed for elementary, middle, or secondary schools or for special content schools—vocational or performing arts. These lists are used most often for opening a new school library media center. School library media specialists and review committees customize these lists to user needs.
2. Publishers' catalogs. These are good starting points for locating specific titles and comparison shopping.
3. Vendors representing one or more publishers. Too little has been said about establishing good relationships with vendors, who have access to demonstration materials and can make them available for review. Naturally, they want to sell their employers' products; however, most are familiar with their competitors' product lines and work collaboratively to help schools secure the most appropriate materials.
4. Bibliographic indexes of subject specific titles with summaries. These indexes are not free and are most cost effective if housed in the district professional library. The same is true of *Books in Print*, in print and non-print formats. Because its contents change significantly from year to year, many districts cannot justify its cost, relying instead on direct communication with publishers to determine a book's status.
5. Publications such as *Publishers Weekly* provide information on the latest releases, current topics, and book reviews.

Methods:
1. Review resources using existing tools. The school library media center staff should gather information concerning contents and cost of considered items and budget allocation figures.
2. Organize a review committee. This may be a district committee for selection of materials to be purchased for several schools or a local committee (the library media advisory committee if one exists) for selection of specific titles or series. The committee should be composed mainly of teachers, representing a cross-section of grade levels and subject areas.
   At the district review, involving large numbers of items, the district supervisor may have items available for on-site preview. If possible, the school committee should have products available for examination. Ask a vendor to make a presentation.
3. Use the material in a classroom setting for an immediate evaluation of its worth. Naturally, this method requires that a faculty member—teacher or library media specialist—preview the item first to determine its suitability for the intended audience.

Preferably, written records of all reviews should be kept in the district media office. Most districts have a preview form for rating an item against evaluative criteria.

Most school libraries use an automated circulation system that requires information to be cataloged in MARC format. **MARC** stands for Machine Readable Cataloging. Machine readable means that a machine such as a computer can read the content of the record. The cataloging record provides details about an item such as the description, main entry, subjects, and classification or call number. Cataloging records follow specific rules as outlined in **AACR2** (Anglo-American Cataloging Rules, Second Edition).

> **Learn more about MARC format**
>
> http://www.loc.gov/marc/umb/

The MARC format is relatively universal and enables a school library to utilize many commercial automation tools. The format allows for unlimited fields, which provide more efficient cataloging for both print and non-print items. Each field is marked with a tag. A tag represents a specific piece of information, i.e. 245 tag lists title information and the 520 tag marks the summary.

> **Learn more about AACR2**
>
> http://130.15.161.74/techserv/cat/Sect02a/c02a2.html

Citing resources used for research or student projects is an important part of teaching students about copyright and fair use of information. When citing resources it is best to follow the preferred format of the instructor. Many online tools can assist students with this process. The tools generally follow one of the following types of bibliographic formats. (Examples given are very general; specific formatting for each style can be much more complex.)

- MLA – Modern Language Association style
1. In text, list the author's last name and page number in parentheses: (Smith 56).
2. Works cited are listed alphabetically by the author's last name in the following format:
Smith, John. *Book Title: Book Subtitle*. Location: Publisher, 2008.

> **Learn more about bibliographic formats**
>
> http://owl.english.purdue.edu/owl/
>
> See Research and Citation link

- APA – American Psychological Association style
1. In text, when the author is not mentioned, a citation would read: (Smith, 2008, p. 56). When the author is mentioned, the abbreviated citation in text would read: (2008, p. 56).
2. The reference listing would be:
Smith, J. (2008). *Book title: Book subtitle*. Location: Publisher.

- Chicago Manual of Style

1. In text, list the author's last name and publication date: (Smith 2008).

2. The bibliography entry would be:

Smith, John. 2008. *Book title: Book subtitle*. Location: Publisher.

Skill 2.3   Selecting equipment, supplies, and services: equipment such as computers and audiovisual equipment, supplies such as disks, services such as on-line services and CD-ROMs

In addition to the general selection criteria, certain other specific criteria must be followed when selecting media and equipment.

Types of media include

1. Printed or display media (pamphlets, handouts, flannel boards, flip charts etc.).
2. Overhead transparencies.
3. DVD-ROM recordings.
4. Audio recordings on CD-ROM.
5. Videotape recordings.
6. Computer software.
7. Online resources.
8. Periodicals

In addition to following the guidelines outlined in the district's overall selection policy, some or all of the following criteria may be applied to the media formats including CD-ROMs, DVDs, software, and online resources.

1. Technical quality. Sound quality, picture focus, font size, screen color, physical dimensions—these characteristics must be technically correct and artistically appealing for the information within to be appreciated and absorbed by the learner.
2. Packaging. Circulating non-print media need to be packaged in reusable containers to protect them from wear and tear.
3. Cost. The advantages of one format over another must be studied for the limits of the current budget, the size of the group to be served, the durability of the product in terms of the investment. Some products may be considered for rental rather than purchase.
4. Applicability. The product should be suitable for available equipment to use it with, appropriate to the climate and environment in which it will be used, and potentially usable with individuals as well as small or large groups.
5. Educational value. If possible, evidence that the selected media format has been tested with learners to prove its value to the learning process should be provided with the product advertisement.

6. Technical specifications. Check the specifications of the software to be sure that it will run on equipment within the school.

Equipment criteria:
With the rapidly changing capabilities of computers and other electronic equipment, it is important to follow district guidelines to ensure compatibility with network services and other devices. Some districts have minimum requirements for purchasing computers and other peripherals.
Criteria for school level equipment purchases could include:
1. Balance. The amount of audiovisual materials, the frequency of need for these materials, and the preference of teachers will influence the number of items to purchase. District guidelines may set minimum levels.
2. Condition of existing equipment. Some years the budget may be needed for replacement of worn or damaged pieces. Some new equipment is essential to keep up with new media formats.

Selection tools:

1. Company catalogs.
2. State or district approved lists.
3. Free services or reduced cost products: ITV, MECC.
4. Preview or observation of products.

Skill 2.4 Acquiring resources: knowledge and evaluation of publishers, jobbers, subscriptions, vendors; knowledge of ordering procedures

Selection of equipment often depends upon the companies represented on the state bid list or local companies with whom the district contracts. Whenever shopping off the bid list, it is advisable to consult the district purchasing agent who may be able to secure better prices than those quoted in company catalogs.

Company catalogs cite specifications of physical dimensions, power needs, etc.

For review of quality and performance use periodicals: *New Media, Technology Review, PC Week, MAC Week, Media and Methods*, and consult with other media professionals.

A number of resources may be used in the selection of print and non-print media.

1. Catalogs from publishers and vendors.
2. Bibliographies in outstanding reference books or textbooks.
3. Lists provided by library associations.
   a. *Selected Films for Young Adults*
   b. *Outstanding Books for the College Bound*
4. Standard catalogs.
   a. *Children's Catalog*
   b. *Elementary School Library Collections*
   c. *Senior High School Library Catalog*
5. Lists of award winners: Caldecott Medal and Newbery Medal.
6. Lists of notable materials in books on children's literature (Pillon, Sutherland, etc.) and library media publications like the *School Library Media Annual.*

Book purchases may be made through various **jobbers**. A jobber buys products from a manufacturer or wholesaler and sells it to retailers. Popular book jobbers are Baker and Taylor, Blackwell Book Services, Coutts Library Services, and Midwest Library Services.

> **Learn more about jobbers**
>
> http://www.google.com/Top/Business/Information_Services/Library_Services/Book_Jobbers/

There are issues that a school library media specialist may run into when purchasing materials for the library. Books may be back ordered or no longer in print and can cause an order to be returned incomplete. There are certain procedures to employ to ensure schools get the most for their money.

- Prepare a list of books using recommended professional reviewing sources such as *School Library Journal, Booklist, H.W. Wilson* publications, etc.
- Provide a "Do Not Exceed" amount rather than add up the value of books ordered.
- Supply vendor with needed information.
  - The Circulation System—Example: Athena or Follett
  - Computer Hardware—MAC or Windows Format
  - Barcode Start #
  - Barcode Symbology—3 of 9
- Check in book orders upon receipt of shipment. It is very important to verify items shipped with items ordered.
- Upload MARC records into library automation system.

Skill 2.5 Organizing resources: MARC records; descriptive cataloging; classification; processing; records management; circulation; automation; and organization of noncataloged materials

The MARC format is relatively universal and enables a school library to utilize many commercial automation tools. The format allows for unlimited fields, which provide more efficient cataloging for both print and non-print items. Each field is marked with a tag. A tag represents a specific piece of information, i.e. 245 tag lists title information and the 520 tag marks the summary.

The MARC format assists in preserving bibliographic integrity. Bibliographic integrity refers to the accuracy and uniformity with which items are cataloged. Following a standard set of international rules, *Anglo-American Cataloguing Rules*, enables users to locate materials equally well in all libraries that subscribe to these rules. To maintain this integrity, catalogers

1. Recognize an **International Standard Bibliographic Description (ISBD)** that establishes the order in which bibliographic elements will appear in catalog entries.
2. Note changes that occur after each five years review of ISBD.
3. Agree to catalog all materials using the AACR standards.

> **Learn more about ISBD**
>
> http://en.wikipedia.org/wiki/International_Standard_Bibliographic_Description

The components of a basic bibliographic record that may be used in **LCC** (Library of Congress Classification) or **DDC** (Dewey Decimal Classification) shelf-list cards or in Online Computer Library Center's MARC records for automated systems are:

1. Call Number. Includes DDC or LCC classification number followed by a book identification identifier (numerals or letters).
2. Author Main Entry Heading. Use name by which author is most commonly known even if that name is a pseudonym.
3. Title and Statement of Responsibility Area. Include title, subtitle, or parallel titles and name(s) of authors, editors, illustrators, translators, or groups functioning in authorship capacity.
4. Edition Statement. Provide ordinal number of edition.
5. Material Specific Details. Used with only four materials (computer files, cartographic materials, printed music, and serials in all formats).
6. Publication and Distribution Area. Include place of publication, name of publisher and copyright date.

> **Learn more about LCC**
>
> http://www.loc.gov/catdir/cpso/lcco/

7. Physical Description Area. Include the extent of the work (number of pages, volumes, or other units); illustrative matter; size/dimensions; and accompanying materials.
8. Series. Provide title of series and publication information if different from statement of responsibility.
9. Notes. Provide information to clarify any other descriptive components, including audiovisual formats or reading levels.
10. Standard numbers. Provide ISBN, ISSN, or LCC number, price, or other terms of availability.

There are three levels of bibliographic description.

1. Level 1 descriptions are the simplest and most appropriate for small or general collections. Although they satisfy AACR standards, they are not considered full records.
2. Level 2 descriptions are more detailed and are used by medium to large libraries where clients use materials for research. Many libraries, including small media centers, use description formats somewhere between Level 1 and Level 2.
3. Level 3 descriptions are full records that require application of every AACR rule. Most major libraries, even the Library of Congress, develop some system just short of full Level 3 cataloging.

OCLC (Online Computer Library Center) bibliographic records (MARC) use both a short form (Level I enhanced) and a long form (Level 2).

It is necessary for all entries to have standardized subject headings. **Sears List of Subject Headings** is generally used in Dewey Decimal Classification while the Library of Congress has its own subject heading list.

> **Learn more about the Sears List of Subject Headings**
>
> http://www.hwwilson.com/print/sears lst_18th.cfm

Many companies that serve libraries provide a service that provides complete MARC records for materials ordered. This is a time saving feature for school library media specialists who would have to hand key all of the MARC tags.

The primary way of determining use of library materials and services is to examine circulation records. With automated systems, it is possible to generate monthly statistics on the number of items circulated. Dividing by the average number of items a user may check out during that circulation period will provide an idea of the number of users who visited the media center.

It is important to be consistent in cataloging procedures as many districts compile the resources of all their media centers into a single online or networked catalog. A catalog that contains listings of materials from several library collections is known as a Union Catalog.

LIBRARY MEDIA

In elementary schools where whole classes may visit on a regular schedule, usage may be tabulated by multiplying class size by the number of visits. In schools with flexible scheduling, keeping a log of visits and the number of participants in each group might result in a truer figure since users may do in-house research, use computers, create media productions, or otherwise use services that do not involve borrowing materials.

Circulation policies and procedures should be flexible to allow ready access and secure to protect borrowers' rights of confidentiality.

The components of circulation procedures:

1. Circulation system. Most circulation systems are automated; this system should:
   a. Be simple to use for convenience of staff as well as to save time for borrowers.
   b. Provide for the loan and retrieval of print and non-print materials and equipment.
   c. Facilitate the collection of circulation statistics.

2. Rules governing circulation:
   a. Length of loan period.
   b. Process for handling overdue materials.
   c. Limitations.
      i. Number of items circulable to individual borrower.
      ii. Overnight loan for special items (vertical file materials, reference books, audiovisual materials or equipment).
      iii. Reserve collections.

3. Rules governing fines for damages or lost materials.

4. Security provisions.
   a. Theft detection devices on print and non-print media.
   b. Straps or lock-downs on equipment transported by cart.

Automated circulation systems have several advantages.

1. Ease and speed of use. Barcodes and scanning devices speed the process. Data is quickly retrievable and saves storage space for cards and card files.
2. Compatible catalog programs. Information on circulation status, descriptions of material type and format, and call numbers are included.
3. Collection evaluation and usage statistics.

TEACHER CERTIFICATION STUDY GUIDE

Some disadvantages include

1. Cost of equipment, service contracts, and annual updates.
2. Power interruptions.
3. Confidentiality of user information.

Inventory is the process of verifying the collection holdings and assessing the collection's physical condition. Its purposes are

1. To indicate lost or missing materials. Identify items for replacement.
2. To reveal strengths and weaknesses in collection. Inventory helps identify areas where numbers of materials do not reflect need.
3. To identify materials needing repair. Periodic preventive maintenance can save major repair or replacement cost.
4. To shape the process of weeding. Outdated and damaged or worn materials would be removed to maintain the integrity of the collection's reputation.

Procedures:

1. Specify when inventory will be conducted. Most schools conduct inventories at the end of the school year. Many districts require that inventory statistics be turned in to the school or district supervisors before media staff vacations.
2. Determine who will conduct inventory. Personnel availability will determine whether inventory will be conducted by professionals, support staff, or some combination, during school hours or during closed time.
3. Examine each item and match it to the holding records. Pull items for repair.
4. Tabulate results and record on forms required by the school or district.

Skill 2.6   Promotion of resources

Establish and nurture an administrative partnership with the principal and district director of media to develop, establish, and fund library program goals. In larger districts that have a district director of media, avenues of support may be clearly defined. In smaller districts, where the media director also handles other administrative duties or where there is no district coordinator, support is based on the lobbying efforts of the school library media specialist. In any case, the principal must be the media center's staunchest ally. Present the annual program goals and implementation procedures to the principal early in the school year for his input and approval. Invite him to participate in faculty in-services and advisory committee meetings. Ask to be included on the school's curriculum planning team.

LIBRARY MEDIA

Exhibit your willingness to assume a leadership role in integrating the library media program into the total school program. Make every attempt to ensure that some phase of the library media program appears in each year's school improvement plan.

Work with the district media director and other school library media specialists to establish and maintain a uniformly excellent district library media program. Continually evaluate the goals and objectives of the school program compared to the district program and matched to the users' needs as identified in annual assessments.

Attend school board meetings. Be aware of all issues affecting the media program, instruction, and the budget. Invite county or area superintendents and school board members to district media meetings to discuss issues and plan improvements. Make yourself and your enthusiasm for the library media program visible.

Read widely in the resources listed in 1.3. A knowledgeable library media specialist is the best human resource in the school. There is perhaps no better promotion for the media center than having students, teachers, and administrators seeking information from the library media center staff.

Attend college courses, in-service training, and professional conferences. Offer to teach night college courses, supervise a library media candidate, offer workshops for school faculty, and make presentations at conferences. But remember to be selective. Never forsake your ethical responsibility to serve patrons by overextending your commitments.

Keep apprised of state certification requirements for certificate renewal and complete renewal requirements (1.9) in a timely manner.

Systematically assess program needs at least annually. Always have available statistics about media center use (5.1), lesson plans or visitation schedules, and written evaluations of instructional activities. Make presentations to School Improvement Committees, parent support groups, or community agencies. Making thorough, accurate reports indicates a well-managed program and encourages maximum support.

COMPETENCY 3.0 INFORMATION ACCESS AND DELIVERY

Skill 3.1 Knowledge of information resources and their uses, both book and nonbook, including electronic

Most libraries contain print resources that fall either into the reference category or the circulating materials category.

Reference materials are generally housed in a special location within the media center. They are there for patrons to use, but are rarely allowed to be checked out and taken home. Reference materials include almanacs, dictionaries, encyclopedias, special sets of books, atlases, and manuals.

Circulating materials are those that can be checked out. They cover a wide range of topics and can include works of non-fiction as well as fiction.

Technology has changed the instructional resources now available to schools. There are many types of resources that can be found in multiple formats. Types of resources that are used in schools can include:

- Overhead transparencies—Overheads are still a viable tool for instruction. Transparencies easily created using computer software and films meant for either inkjet or laser printers.
- Multimedia Presentations—As technology has become more readily available teachers use multimedia presentations to accentuate material being presented to students. The format is often more appealing than transparencies, but availability of equipment can be an issue.

- Audio recordings—Older formats such as vinyl records have been replaced by cassette tapes then CDs. Podcasts or computerized records are currently a popular format. These recordings can be played directly from the computer or downloaded onto various devices.
- Video recordings—Filmstrips have given way to videotaped presentations. Video is more animated than its predecessor and can be found in various formats such as video tape, DVDs, Blu-ray discs, and video streamed from online sources. \
- Print material—Libraries are still stocked with books that can be checked out from its location. Books can also be found in audio format as well as electronic formats called ebooks.
- Computer Software—Many learning opportunities are supported through the use of computer software stored on CD-ROMs. Schools physically store the software on either a single machine or it is loaded on a server for the sharing of the software across the school's network. Special licenses are required for network use.
- Online Programs—Many resources once housed within the walls of the media center can now be accessed online. Some resources are subscription based but are still considerably cheaper than upgrading software on CD-ROMs. One downfall of this format can be the space it takes up on the districts bandwidth. Online resources containing a great deal of video can cause a network to perform considerably slower.

A wide variety of resources is available online to assist school library media specialists with providing access to current information. Below are listed several information resources. More online resources can be found in 3.5.

Periodical Directories
Ulrich's International Periodicals Directory
- complete and current reference for select periodicals and serials
- information collected from over 80,000 worldwide serials publishers
- contains annuals, continuations, conference proceedings

SIRS Enduring Issues
- print versions contains eight volumes and 32 topics
- highlights the best articles published during the preceding year

Public Affairs Information Service (PAIS)
- references over 553,300 journal articles, books, documents directories and reports
- offered online

Indexes

The New York Times
- assists with locating articles and information printed in the *New York Times* newspaper
- searchable by topic and uses the words "See also" to suggest other subject headings

Professional Journals

The Library Quarterly
- scholarly research regarding all areas of librarianship

School Library Media Research
- published by American Association of School Librarians
- the successor to *School Library Media Quarterly Online*
- purpose is to provide research concerning the management, implementation, and evaluation of school library media programs

Library Trends
- explores critical trends in professional librarianship
- includes practical applications and literature reviews

Library Power
- research study that proved the viability of school libraries as a vehicle to promote student achievement

American Libraries
- published by the American Library Association
- provides the latest news and updates from the association

School Library Journal
- serves school and public librarians who work with young
- provides information needed to integrate libraries into all aspects of the school curriculum
- provides review of currently published children and young adult books
- provides resources to become effective technology leaders
- provides resources to assist with collection development

VOYA (Voice of Youth Advocates)
- focuses on librarians and educators working with young adults
- founded by Dorothy M. Broderick and Mary K. Chelton

School Library Media Activities Monthly Magazine
- designed for K-8 school library media specialists
- focuses on collaboratively planned units with teachers
- stresses importance of introducing reference materials

TEACHER CERTIFICATION STUDY GUIDE

Knowledge Quest
- published by The American Association of School Librarians
- designed to assist with the development of school library media programs

Skill 3.2 Knowledge of literature: genres, awards, and review sources

In addition to the works of Carlsen, Donelson, Huck, and Sutherland, all of which contain excellent information on children's/adolescent interests and needs, the school library media specialist can rely on lists of titles published in other resources. The *School Library Media Annual* includes Caldecott and Newbery Medal winners and notable materials lists such as

1. Notable Books for Children—Association for Library Service to Children of ALA.
2. Children's Reviewers Choice—Booklist.
3. Children's Choices—The Children's Book Council.
4. Best Books for Young Adults—Young Adult Services Division of ALA.
5. Young Adult Reviewers Choice—Booklist.
6. Notable Children's Films—ALSC.
7. Selected Films for Young Adults—YASD.

Bookseller John Newbery was the first to publish literature for children on any scale in the second half of 18th century England, the great outpouring of children's literature came 100 years later in the Victorian Age. Novels such as Charles Dickens's *Oliver Twist*, Robert Louis Stevenson's *Treasure Island*, and Rudyard Kipling's *Jungle Book*, though not written for children alone, have become classics in children's literature. These books not only helped them understand the world they lived in but satisfied their sense of adventure.

> **Learn more about The Newberry Award**
>
> http://www.ala.org/Template.cfm?Section=bookmediaawards&template=/ContentManagement/ContentDisplay.cfm&ContentID=149311

The Newbery Medal Award was created in honor of John Newbery in 1922. This award is presented to an author of the most notable children's or young adult work of fiction.

Newbery Medal awarded books for the past fifteen years are:
2008 – **Good Masters! Sweet Ladies! Voices from a Medieval Village** written by Laura Amy Schlitz, illustrated by Robert Byrd
2007 – **The Higher Power of Lucky** written by Susan Patron, illustrated by Matt Phelan
2006 – **Criss Cross** by Lynne Rae Perkins
2005 – **Kira-Kira** by Cynthia Kadohata
2004 – **The Tale of Despereaux: Being the Story of a Mouse, a Princess, Some Soup, and a Spool of Thread** written by Kate DiCamillo, illustrated by Timothy Basil Ering

2003 – *Crispin: The Cross of Lead* by Avi
2002 – *A Single Shard* by Linda Sue Park
2001 – *A Year Down Yonder* by Richard Peck
2000 – *Bud, Not Buddy* by Christopher Paul Curtis
1999 – *Holes* by Louis Sachar
1998 – *Out of the Dust* by Karen Hesse
1997 – *The View from Saturday* by E.L. Konigsburg
1996 – *The Midwife's Apprentice* by Karen Cushman
1995 – *Walk Two Moons* by Sharon Creech
1994 – *The Giver* by Lois Lowry

Many of the most popular books for children in the late 19th and early 20th century were translations of foreign favorites like Andrew Lang's *The Blue Fairy Book* (and its rainbow of successors); Astrid Lindgren's *Pippi Longstocking*; Johanna Spyri's *Heidi*; and Jean de Brunhoff's *Babar* series. Titles in English such as Beatrix Potter's *Tales*, A.A. Milne's *Winnie the Pooh* tales, and Kenneth Grahame's *Wind in the Willows* have remained popular into the 1990s. The beauty of many of these books is their universality of appeal.

In recognition of outstanding translations of children's books, the Mildred L. Batchelder Award was created in 1966. This award goes to the publisher that is responsible for translating the work into English.

Children's/adolescent literature of the last 50 years has grown to thousands of new titles per year and many tend to the trendy, the authors and publishers being very aware of the market and the social changes affecting their products. Books are selected for libraries because of their social, psychological, and intellectual value. Collections must also contain materials that recognize cultural and ethnic needs. Because so many popular titles, especially in the young adult area, deal with controversial subjects, school library media specialists are faced with juggling the preferences of their student patrons with the need to provide worthwhile literature and maintain intellectual freedom in the face of increasing censorship. Books such as Robert Cormier's *Chocolate War*, *Beyond the Chocolate War,* and *Fade* deal with the darker side of teen life. Paul Zindel's *Pigman* and *The Undertaker's Gone Bananas* deal with the stresses in teen life with a touch of humor.

Books of the young child reader teach about his relationships to the world around him and to other people and things in that world. They help him learn how things operate and how to overcome his fears. Like the still popular fairy tales of previous centuries, some of today's popular children's books are fantasies or allegories, such as Robert O'Brien's *Mrs. Frisby and the Rats of NIMH*.

Popular books for preadolescents deal more with establishing relationships with members of the opposite sex (Sweet Valley High series) and learning to cope with their changing bodies, personalities, or life situations as in Judy Blume's *Are You There, God? It's Me, Margaret*. Adolescents are still interested in the fantasy and science fiction genres as well as popular juvenile fiction. Middle school students still read the *Little House on the Prairie* series and the mysteries of the Hardy Boys and Nancy Drew. Teens value the works of Emily and Charlotte Brontë, Willa Cather, Jack London, William Shakespeare, and Mark Twain as much as those of Piers Anthony, S.E. Hinton, Madeleine L'Engle, Stephen King, and J.R.R. Tolkien because they're fun to read whatever their underlying worth may be.

Well-known writers of children's fiction include Betsy Byars, Susan Cooper, Shirley Hughes, Sheila Solomon Klass, Elizabeth George Speare, Gary K. Wolf, and Laurence Yep. Children's poets include Nancy Larrick, Maurice Sendak, and Shel Silverstein.

Fiction writers popular with young adolescents include Judy Blume, Alice Childress, Beverly Cleary, Roald Dahl, Virginia Hamilton, Kathryn Lasky, Lois Lowry, Robin McKinley, Katherine Paterson, Teresa Tomlinson, and Bill Wallace.

Popular genres and authors in children's literature include:.
1. Fantasy: Piers Anthony, Ursula K. Le Guin, and Anne McCaffrey
2. Horror: V.C. Andrews, Stephen King
3. Juvenile fiction: Judy Blume, Robert Cormier, Rosa Guy, Virginia Hamilton, S.E. Hinton, M.E. Kerr, Harry Mazer, Norma Fox Mazer, Robert Newton Peck, Cynthia Voigt, and Paul Zindel
4. Science fiction: Isaac Asimov, Ray Bradbury, Arthur C. Clarke, Frank Herbert, Larry Niven, and H.G. Wells
5. Folk Tales: spoken stories that are passed down through generations
6. Historical Fiction
7. Picture books and picture story books

> **Learn more about popular genres of children's literature**
>
> http://www.uleth.ca/edu/currlab/handouts/genres.html

Books for younger children generally include picture books. Notable children's book author/illustrators include Marcia Brown, Leo and Diane Dillon, Barbara Cooney, Nonny Hogrogian, David Macaulay, Emily Arnold McCully, Allen Say, Maurice Sendak, Chris Van Allsburg, and David Wiesner.

Each year an outstanding illustrator of a children's book is honored for his or her outstanding work by being presented with the **Caldecott Medal**. This award was created in honor of Randolph Caldecott and is distributed annually by the *Association for Library Service for Children*. It was first presented in 1938.

> **Learn more about the Caldecott Medal**
>
> http://www.ala.org/Template.cfm?Section=bookmediaawards&template=/ContentManagement/ContentDisplay.cfm&ContentID=164637

Award winners for the past fifteen years are:
- 2008 – **The Invention of Hugo Cabret** by Brian Selznick
- 2007 – **Flotsam** by David Wiesner
- 2006 – **The Hello, Goodbye Window** illustrated by Chris Raschka, text by Norton Juster
- 2005 – **Kitten's First Full Moon** by Kevin Henkes
- 2004 – **The Man Who Walked Between the Towers** by Mordicai Gerstein
- 2003 – **My Friend Rabbit** by Eric Rohmann
- 2002 – **The Three Pigs** by David Wiesner
- 2001 – **So You Want to Be President?** illustrated by David Small, text by Judith St. George
- 2000 – **Joseph Had a Little Overcoat** by Simms Taback
- 1999 – **Snowflake Bentley** illustrated by Mary Azarian, text by Jacqueline Briggs Martin
- 1998 – **Rapunzel** by Paul O. Zelinsky
- 1997 – **Golem** by David Wisniewski
- 1996 – **Officer Buckle and Gloria** by Peggy Rathmann
- 1995 – **Smoky Night** illustrated by David Diaz, text by Eve Bunting
- 1994 – **Grandfather's Journey** by Allen Say; text by Walter Lorraine

Other awards have come about in recent years. The *Coretta Scott King Award* is presented to African American authors and illustrators for their outstanding educational contributions.

The Laura Ingalls Wilder award honors an author or illustrator whose books have made a significant and lasting contribution to literature for children. The books must be published in the United States.

> **Learn more about other book awards**
>
> http://www.ala.org/Template.cfm?Section=bookmediaawards

The Mildred L. Batchelder Award, first presented to its namesake in 1954, is a bronze medal award that honors an author or illustrator whose books were translated into English and published in the United States and have made a lasting contribution for literature for children.

Skill 3.3   Knowledge of current technologies

Technology is constantly changing and has a major impact on the role of the school library media specialist and his/her role in the learning community. Computers that used to contain diskette drives are now giving way to those with CD-RW or DVD-RW drives. Almost all peripherals connect via USB (Universal Serial Bus) ports and are Plug and Play devices, meaning they install and can run automatically.

Overhead projectors and filmstrips have given way to LCD projectors, laptops, document cameras and other presentation devices. Video can be edited and produced using a computer and be recorded to CD-ROMs or DVDs. Audio can be produced to be played on CD-ROMs or online as a podcast.

As technology changes, the school library media specialist must keep abreast of the new technologies available so that she/he may train students and staff in their use.

Now they must also teach both teachers and students how to use computers and their applications. If the media center has only computers for the automated catalog, the instruction is usually done for individuals or small groups as they need to locate materials. Peer instruction can be very efficient in using automated indexes. Student library aides or volunteers can assist with informal instruction.

If the media center has an attached computer lab, operation of and instruction in the lab may also become the specialist's responsibility. Support staff or paraprofessionals can supervise laboratory activities and the classroom teacher can provide content instruction and/or operational procedure.

Media production rooms where school wide television broadcasts are created are found in many schools. The school library media specialist must also learn how to use video equipment, production equipment, and editing equipment or software.

In addition, the media specialist is also often expected to be a technician responsible for the cleaning and maintenance of not only the technologies in the media center but throughout the school. In small districts, technical assistance may be provided by the district computer department or through an external contractor or the technical division of the company from whom the technology was purchased. Larger districts may have a technical support staff that travels from school to school. Rarely does any individual school have enough professional or paraprofessional personnel to cover all responsibilities adequately.

Furthermore, the school library media specialist is expected to serve as technology consultant, advising teachers on hardware and software to serve their instructional needs.

One common technical support issue that arises in older machines with a floppy drive is the boot disk error. This occurs when a diskette has been left in the disk drive when the computer is booted. To correct this error, simply eject the disk and follow the instructions on screen.

With the array of file types school library media specialists must deal with, it is important to understand what the file types stand for.
- .jpg or .jpeg – (joint photographic experts group) picture file
- .gif – (graphics interchange format) picture file
- .bmp – (bitmap) picture file
- .png – (portable network graphics) picture file
- .doc – document file
- .txt – text file
- .pdf – (portable document format)
- .html – (hypertext markup language) web page file

The ALA/AECT guidelines recommend a division of responsibilities, but financial considerations are often used as the final determining factor in making personnel decisions. It becomes the school library media specialist's task to prioritize her responsibilities. Too often the time-consuming tasks of introducing and maintaining new technologies overshadow other responsibilities.

Development of viable technology plans has been a concern at the local, district, and state levels. Initially, technology plans involved determining the number of pieces of hardware to buy, the installation cost and procedures, and the physical maintenance system. How they would be used for instruction or information gathering was seldom addressed. Only recently has the educational soundness of planning before hardware purchase become a universal concern.

Long-range technology plans may evolve from district plans for school-to-school connectivity and resource sharing plans as well as from goals that match the local school goals. Preferably, these goals would be included in the School Improvement Plan, and often it is the library media specialist who chairs the technology committee. The 3-5 year plan should address the learning objectives and the technology needed to meet those objectives. It should also project the cost of hardware, software, phone time charges, peripherals, etc. Finally, it should prioritize the goals. The short-range plan should address one or more priorities and the following related factors:

1. Immediate cost and funding sources.
2. Implementation. What type of hardware, software, and peripherals should be purchased to meet the goals? Are there networking considerations—cabling, electrical outlets, surge protection? Are there concerns about the use of certain technologies—multi-user contracts, dedicated phone lines, monitoring student access to Internet sites?
3. Flexibility. Does the technology have durability and potential future use? Is it upgradeable or does it have possible use elsewhere if new or upgraded technology becomes available? Can the goals be adjusted easily as needs change?

Attending workshops and conferences is part of the library media specialist's continuing education.

National and state organizations conduct annual conventions (ALA, AECT, AASL). Some districts also conduct local conferences on in-service days. These conferences offer two major benefits:

1. Workshops in innovations in the field and the use of emerging technologies are conducted by experts.
2. Vendors from media and equipment companies display the latest in their product lines.

Skill 3.4 Knowledge of the information retrieval processes: search strategies, evaluative techniques

Information retrieval is the process of searching, recovering, and interpreting information from large amounts of stored data.

With the vast amount of information available to library patrons, it is important that they know how to locate information quickly and easily. Whether using in-house resources such as an automated circulation systems and CD-ROM database or searching for information online, effective search strategies must be employed.

The main type of search is a keyword search where the user searches for information using specific terms. To aid in this type of search certain operators called **Boolean Operators** can narrow topics. Popular operators include:
- AND – ex. lions and tigers – both words must be found in the searched text
- AND NOT – ex. lions AND NOT tigers – lions must be listed, but do not return listings that contain the word tigers
- OR – ex. lions OR tigers – may contain either word

> **Learn more about Boolean Operators**
>
> http://www.internettutorials.net/boolean.html

Reference requests are of three types depending on the depth of the question and the scope of the search. Some very simple questions can lead to complex searches, however.

1. Ready reference request. These requests usually require a limited search in standard reference books (encyclopedias, atlases, almanacs) or electronic databases (SIRS Researcher, Grolier's Encyclopedia, 3D Atlas, or American Heritage Dictionary and Thesaurus). The request is satisfied by directing the requestor to the exact sources in which the information may be found. Occasionally, a seemingly simple question cannot be answered quickly and thus necessitates a higher-level search.

    If the library carries the *Who's Who in America* and *Who Was Who in America* series, an American is easy to identify. However, most school library media centers do not purchase biographical dictionaries of foreign persons unless they were noteworthy in a particular profession. *Who's Who in Science, Current Biography, Webster's Biographical Dictionary, British Writers Before 1900* are some helpful resources.

2. Specific need requests. These requests are the most frequently addressed and may range from merely steering the requestor to a card catalog, index, or other bibliographic aid if the user is familiar with those tools. It may become a lengthy project if the resource must be found outside the school or if the user needs instruction in using search tools and locating the resources.

    A student debater may want to know which resources would give statistics about teen pregnancy. A teacher may ask which books and periodicals have the best articles on inclusion of special education students.

    The answer to specific need questions entails locating the resources by identifying the proper search tools (card catalog, the *Reader's Guide to Periodical Literature*, or automated indexes like InfoTrac or NewsBank).

3. Research request. This question is encountered most often in secondary school or university/academic libraries. The search is broader in scope and requires more time. Any specific need request could be expanded into a research request.

    The debater may be preparing a portfolio for a contest and need photocopies of available material. A teacher taking a college course may ask the school library media specialist to pull periodical articles relating to inclusion. These requests may require using on-line databases and research queries outside the library media center.

Research services are gaining wider need as users are confronted with great amounts of information and less time to conduct their searches.

The World Wide Web has brought information directly to the end user. Such an abundance of information makes it important to teach students and adults how to discriminate the good from the bad. When looking at online information there are key points to consider.

1. How accurate is the information?
2. Who wrote the information? What authority do they have on the subject?
3. What type of site is it? Commercial is .com, organizational is .org, educational is .edu, governmental is .gov, television is .tv, and so on.
4. How current is the information?
5. Is it easy to navigate or does it require special software to load?

Skill 3.5 **Information resources sharing: interlibrary loan, networks, programming, information and communication technology, LANs, school/public library cooperation**

Resource sharing has always been an integral part of education. Before the technology revolution, the sharing was done within schools or departments and between teachers. Now it is possible to access information around the world.

Resource sharing is a way of

1. Providing a broader information base to enable users to find and access the resources that provide the needed information.
2. Reducing or containing media center budgets.
3. Establishing cooperation with other resource providers that encourage mutual planning and standardization of control.

Resource sharing systems:

1. **Interlibrary loan**. The advent of computer databases has simplified the process of locating sources in other libraries.
   Local public library collections can be accessed from terminals in the media center. Physical access depends on going to the branch where the material is housed.

> Learn more about interlibrary loan
>
> http://www.ala.org/ala/alalibrary/libraryfactsheet/alalibraryfactsheet8.cfm

2. **Networking systems**.
   Sharing information has become even easier with the use of network services. Files can be shared and accessed from room to room, school to school and city to city. Resources can be shared within a small geographic location such as a school by the use of a local area network or LAN. A wide area network or WAN is used to communicate over a larger area such as a school district or city.

   > Learn more about networks
   >
   > http://en.wikipedia.org/wiki/Computer_network

   a. E-mail allows educators to communicate across the state.
   b. On-line services (Internet providers) offer access to a specific menu of locations. Monthly fees and/or time charges must be budgeted.
   c. Individual city or county network systems. These are community sponsored networks, often part of the public library system, which provides Internet access for the price of a local phone call. A time limit usually confines an individual search to allow more users access.
   d. On-line continuing education programs offer courses/degrees through at-home study. Large school districts provide lessons for homebound students or home school advocates.
   e. Bulletin boards allow individuals or groups to converse electronically with persons in another place.
3. Telecommunications. Using telephone and television as the media for communication, telecommunications is used primarily for distance learning. Universities or networks of universities (for example, the University of South Carolina and a consortium in North Carolina) provide workshops, conferences, and college credit courses for educators as well as courses for senior high school students in subjects that could not generate adequate class counts in their home schools. Large school districts offer broadcast programming for homebound/home school students.

   The advantage is that students are provided with a phone number so they can interact with the instructors or information providers.

Partnerships between school and public libraries can broaden the access students have to resources and information. One entity becomes and extension of the other. Common practices within these partnerships may include:

1. Inter-library loan. Items can be checked out and shared by each library. Having two collections to pull from provides a greater array of resources available for students and public library patrons.
2. Public librarians visiting the school and conducting special programs. This could include story time activities for younger students or an appearance during an assembly or special program to share the happenings at the public library.

3. School assignments sent to and posted at the public library. This allows the public library to pull resources for research topics or special school projects.

Skill 3.6 Online resources and databases

Technology has brought information directly to the end user. With such an abundance of information it is important to teach students and adults how to discriminate the good from the bad. When looking at online information there are key points to consider.

1. How accurate is the information?
2. Who wrote the information? What authority do they have on the subject?
3. What type of site is it? Commercial is .com, organizational is .org, educational is .edu, government is .gov, television is .tv, and so on.
4. How current is the information?
5. Is it easy to navigate or does it require special software to load?

There are many trusted sources of information that librarians use regularly, some of which were discussed in 3.1. A few examples include:

SIRS Discoverer
- general reference resource for students in grades 1-9
- helps to develop research
- contains a database of over 1600 articles and government documents
- over 9000 educational links

Readers' Guide Full Text, Mega Edition
- current events coverage
- provides periodicals for research

KidsConnect
- spin-off from iConnect
- guides students through four phases of research

KQWeb
- Created by the American Association of School Librarians
- Online companion to their printed journal
- Contains online content not found in the printed text

EBSCO
- provides print and electronic journal subscription services
- provides research database development and production,
- provides online access to more than 150 databases and thousands of e-journals

Questia
- subscription based online library of books, periodicals, newspapers, and encyclopedias

NICEM
- invaluable resource for people who need to identify, locate, and catalog audiovisual products of an educational, documentary, or informative nature.
- audiovisual database is the world's leading source of information for non-print educational and training materials.

Skill 3.7   Distance learning

The school library media center can play an essential role in providing distance learning opportunities. **Distance learning** takes place in any situation where the student and the instructor are in separate locations. The learning can take place in real time and be interactive or can be pre-recorded and viewed at a different time. The teaching may take place in an online venue such as the widely used Blackboard where must of the class discussion occurs during chat sessions or via discussion board. Benefits of distance learning include:

> **Learn more about distance learning**
>
> http://www.ala.org/ala/acrl/acrlstandards/guidelinesdistancelearning.cfm

- Flexibility – students can access and respond to information outside of a normal schedule
- Increased opportunity – distance learning may provide learning experiences for students that may not be possible in their current location
- Multi-sensory experience – distance learning opportunities may include video, digital images, and audio, thus reaching a variety of learning styles.
- Affordability – it may be more cost effective to take advantage of a distance learning class than to hire a teacher to teach only a few students
- Instruction for homebound students

School library media coordinators can take advantage of distance learning activities to increase student access to resources. Not only are distance learning classes offered by colleges, universities, and other secondary education entities, but programs provided by museums, science organizations and other public venues as well. When the school library media specialist collaborates with these units they can increase student access not only to information but to the specialists who provide such information.

When considering distance learning opportunities it is crucial to consider the technology needed to make it a success. One mode of instructional delivery is through video conferencing. When working with large groups an information highway room that is equipped with multiple video cameras, microphones and a large screen video display may be used. For smaller groups or one-on-one delivery a web camera used in conjunction with special software may be just as effective as a larger system. With all of these tools it is necessary to make sure that the computing equipment meets minimum requirements and that there is enough bandwidth to support a large volume of data being sent along the network. Bandwidth would be the speed in which data can be transferred.

Through all of this the school library media coordinator oversees both the technical and instructional pieces to ensure students have every advantage possible.

Skill 3.8 Equal access for all learners: availability of collection services, facilities, and staff; circulation, hours, physical arrangement of the media center

Each school has a unique population of students. The school library media coordinator must collaborate with both regular and special education teachers to find resources that accommodate a wide array of student needs. There are physical conditions that need to be addressed such as the arrangement of furniture and aisles wide enough for wheelchair access. Other physical considerations could include adequate lighting or magnifying devices for visually impaired students and appropriate shelf height for reaching for materials from a wheelchair.

Whether remodeling an existing media center or building a new one, it is important to take into consideration the **American Disabilities Act** regulations. Key documents include:

- ADA Accessibility Guidelines for Buildings and Facilities (ADAAG)
- Americans with Disabilities Act
- Telecommunications Act of 1996 (Section 255)

Learn more about the American Disabilities Act

http://www.ala.org/ala/washoff/contactwo/oitp/emailtutorials/accessibilitya/03.cfm

These documents outline the guidelines for furniture height, aisle width (42 inches), and aisle space around the circulation desk and card catalog.

TEACHER CERTIFICATION STUDY GUIDE

To promote equal access to services the school library media coordinator should plan activities that allow all students to participate successfully. Post rules and signs in large print using pictures and the Braille alphabet. These reminders and cues provide assistance for easily distracted students. Special education teachers may be able to provide additional insight when planning services, physical layout and collections.

Student abilities will influence collection decisions as well. Braille or large print books can be effective for visually-impaired students. Auditory books or software that will read web pages and scanned text can be helpful to students with hearing difficulties.

The use of technology can enhance student access to resources. Some examples include:

- Special computing devices for those with mobility issues are needed to make technology accessible for these students. These devices can be activated by moving a single muscle, blinking or other function.

- Many software programs such as Microsoft Word come with built in accommodations.

- Specialized software that will translate typed text into Braille, sign language, or a different languages.
-
- Using digital technology to synthesize audio, work with digital images and video.

- Using the Internet to take virtual field trips.

Skill 3.9   Scheduling

In today's world, information is available 24/7. School libraries need to modify their scheduling practices so that students and staff can have access to resources at the point of need. This may involve having extended hours, providing remote access to resources, and providing a flexible schedule during the school day.

Providing resources to students and staff beyond the extent of the normal school day is increasingly important. Extended hours allow students to work on research projects or complete schoolwork.

Remote access to information is important to both students and parents. Providing access to online encyclopedias, periodicals, books, and other school resources can involve parents and keep them informed of school resources.

In a flexibly scheduled school library students and staff have access to resources at the point of need. The library media specialist is free to collaboratively plan with them and a schedule is created from the planning sessions. There are no regularly scheduled classes. As a result, the schedule will change from day to day and week to week.

With a flexible schedule, teachers may schedule their classes to come to the library several days in a row for the amount of time they need. Students may come to the library to work individually on projects or they may come to work with small groups of students. A flexible schedule allows students from multiple classes to work in the library at once.

Skill 3.10 Library media center environment

A student-centered media center begins by providing access to resources in an environment that is both interesting and inviting. The space should be well-organized and clearly labeled so that resources can be located. It should have a welcoming atmosphere that entices students and staff to come to the media center to learn.

The school library media specialist is crucial to the development of a climate that encourages learning. To provide such as atmosphere the school library media specialist must be willing to:

- promote the program as a wonderful place for learning
- arrange materials so that they are easy to locate
- set flexible schedules that allow for just in time learning
- be eager to work with students and staff
- maintain an attractive and inviting space
- collaborate with school staff and students

Skill 3.11 Ethical and legal concerns surrounding use of information, such as copyrights in all formats and confidentiality

The advent of technology that made copying print and non-print media efficient poses serious concerns for educators who unwittingly or otherwise violate copyright law on a regular basis. Regardless of their intentions to provide their students access to materials that may be too costly for mass purchase, educators must understand the reasons for copyright protection and they must, by example, ensure the upholding of that protection.

There are many fine publications that clarify copyright law for educators. In many instances, school districts endorse these publications or provide their own concise summarizes for reference. Though all educators should be cognizant of the law, it becomes the responsibility of the school library media specialist to help inform colleagues and monitor the proper application of the law.

Actually, educators have the benefit of greater leeway in copying than any other group. Many print instructional materials carry statements that allow production of multiple copies for classroom use, provided they adhere to the "Guidelines for Classroom Copying in Nonprofit Educational Institutions." Teachers may duplicate enough copies to provide one per student per course provided that they meet the tests of brevity, spontaneity, and cumulative effect.

> **Learn more about copyright and fair use guidelines**
>
> http://www.copyright.gov
> &
> http://www.copyright.gov/fls/fl102.html

1. Brevity test:
   Poetry — suggested maximum 250 words.
   Prose — one complete essay, story, or article less than 2500 words or excerpts of no more than 1000 words or 10% of the work, whichever is less. (Children's books with text under 2500 words may not be copied in their entirety. No more than two pages containing 10% of the text may be copied.)
   Illustration — charts, drawings, cartoons, etc. are limited to one per book or periodical article.
2. Spontaneity test: Normally copying that does not fall under the brevity test requires publisher's permission for duplication. However, allowances are made if "the inspiration and decision to use the work" occur too soon prior to classroom use for permission to be sought in writing.
3. Cumulative effect test: Even in the case of short poems or prose, it is preferable to make only one copy. However, three short items from one work are allowable during one class term. Reuse of copied material from term to term is expressly forbidden. Compilation of works into anthologies to be used in place of purchasing texts is prohibited.
   Copyright legislation has existed in the United States for more than 100 years. Conflicts over copyright were settled in the courts. The 1976 Copyright Act, especially section 107 dealing with Fair Use, created legislative criteria to follow based on judicial precedents. In 1978, when the law took effect, it set regulations for duration and scope of copyright, specified author rights, and set monetary penalties for infringement.
   The statutory penalty may be waived by the court for an employee of a non-profit educational institution where the employee can prove fair use intent.

Fair use, especially important to educators, is meant to create a balance between copyright protection and the needs of learners for access to protected material. Fair use is judged by the purpose of the use, the nature of the work (whether creative or informational), the quantity of the work for use, and the market effect.

In essence, if a <u>portion</u> of a work is used to benefit the learner with no intent to deprive the author of his profits, fair use is granted. Recently, Fair Use has been challenged most in cases of videotaping off-air of television programs. Basic guidelines for this include showing the program within 10 days of recording and erasing the tape by the 45th day. Specific guidelines that affect copying audiovisual materials and computer software are too numerous to delineate. Most distributors place written regulations in the packaging of these products. Allowances for single back-up copies in the event of damage to the original are granted.

Computer software presents additional challenges with respect to copyright and fair use. Permissions, rights and restrictions for software, such as the number of computers where the software can be loaded, are listed in the form of a license.

Section 108 is pertinent to libraries in that it permits reproducing a single copy of an entire work if no financial gain is derived, if the library is public or archival, and if the copyright notice appears on all copies.

In any event in which violation of the law is a concern, the safest course of action is to seek written permission from the publisher of the copyrighted work. If permission is granted, a copy of that permission should accompany any duplicates.

When a suspected infringement of copyright is brought to the attention of the school library media specialist, she should follow certain procedures.

1. Determine if a violation has in effect occurred. Never accuse or report alleged instances to a higher authority without verification.
2. If an instance is verified, tactfully inform the violator of the specific criteria to use so that future violations can be avoided. Presented properly, the information will be accepted as constructive.
3. If advice is unheeded and further infractions occur, bring them to the attention of the teacher's supervisor—a team leader or department chair—who can handle the matter as an evaluation procedure.
4. Inform the person who has reported the alleged violation of the procedures being used.

COMPETENCY 4.0 LEARNING AND TEACHING

Skill 4.1   Curriculum integration and development

This objective can be best achieved if there are existing scope and sequences in other curricular areas. Information skills, like any other content, should not be taught in isolation if they are to be retained and practiced. If no printed sequentials exist, consult with teachers and/or team leaders about planning activities cooperatively to teach information and content skills concurrently.

Teaming with teachers will also meet their instructional objectives. Media specialists need to match resources to those objectives as well as suggest means for using media to demonstrate student skills mastery. Achievement of the design of resource-based teaching units with supplemental or total involvement of the library media center resources and services satisfy levels 9 and 10 of **Loertscher's eleven level taxonomy**, which assumes the active involvement of the school library media specialist in the total school program.

Finally, the self-esteem of students and teachers who learn information management skills is as significant as the information acquisition.

> Learn more about Loertscher's Taxonomies
>
> http://www.ils.unc.edu/daniel/242/Taxonomies.html

A suggested procedure for incorporation follows:

Preparation:
1. Secure any printed scope and sequences from content areas.
2. Meet with team leaders or department chairs early in the year to plan an integrated, sequential program.
3. Attend department or grade-level meetings with specific time devoted to orienting teachers to available resources and services. Plan the best time to schedule orientations for entry level students and reviews for reinforcement.

Implementation:
1. Conduct planned lessons. Distribute copies of objectives, activities, and resources.
2. Review search strategies and challenge students to broaden the scope of resources used to locate information.
3. Provide adequate time for students to carry out lesson activities using media center resources.

Evaluation:
1. Solicit feedback from both students and teachers.
2. Incorporate suggestions into lesson plans.

In most states, basic skills are identified at the grade level for appropriate introduction. Then, objectives are specified at each successive level to review, reinforce, or expand those skills.

For example, the skill of organization dealing with the card catalog is introduced in Grade Levels K-2 as the ability to identify the location and purpose of the card catalog. In Grade Levels 3-4 the skill is expanded to identify the arrangement of and locate information in the card catalog. Grade Levels 5-6 require applying filing rules to locating materials, Grade Levels 7-8 require recognizing using added entry cards, and Grade Levels 9-12 require identifying different catalog formats and classification systems. (Since most schools have gone to automated cataloging in recent years, identification and use of automated formats should be integrated into the continuum.)

The wording of some skills remain the same in all levels. Examples include those concerning selection and use of equipment and accessories and organizing and presenting information/ideas by designing/producing materials.

The types of equipment and material change from filmstrips and finger puppets in K-2 to advanced video equipment and research papers in 9-12. The skill is introduced in K-2 and reviewed, reinforced, and expanded at subsequent grade levels. Using appropriate sources to locate information is introduced at Grade Levels 3-4 with using dictionaries, encyclopedias, and telephone directories; expanded to include atlases, almanacs, periodicals, etc. at Grade Levels 5-6; indexes, yearbooks, specialized dictionaries at Grade Levels 7-8; and handbooks, thesauri, computerized references, and government documents at Grade Levels 9-12.

Some skills are introduced and appear at only one level: identifying the concept of intellectual freedom is introduced as an appreciation skill in Grades 7-8.

Some districts adopt or adapt this DOE scope and sequence according to student ability levels, availability of resources, and other program or facility factors. Each school library media specialist must determine where her students are in sequence prior to planning a teaching strategy.

Instructional planning for the school library media specialist is the process of effectively integrating library skills instruction into the curriculum.

Methods of **instructional planning**:

1. Identify content. Teachers create a list of instructional objectives for specific classes. Library media specialists, using state and local scope and sequence, prepare a list of objectives for teaching information skills.
2. Specify learning objectives. Teachers and library media specialists working together should merge the list of objectives
3. Examine available resources.
4. Determine instructional factors:
    a. Learner styles.
    b. Teaching techniques and teacher and library media specialist division of responsibilities in the lesson implementation.
    c. Student groupings. Consider abilities, special needs, etc.
5. Pretest.
6. Determine activities to meet objectives.
7. Select specific resources and support agencies.
8. Implement the unit.
9. Evaluate.
10. Revise the objectives and/or activities.

Recognizing curriculum changes requires

1. Analysis of current literature and national or state legislation and guidelines.
2. Study of the existing school and district curriculum and its reflection on current standards and future trends.
3. Consultation with local and district curriculum planners and participation in workshops or programs that address curriculum change.

School library media specialists should be more involved in curriculum planning than current research indicates, both on school and district curriculum teams. Sometimes principals must be coaxed into including school library media professionals in curriculum planning because they occasionally forget that media professionals are technically teaching professionals. The school library media specialist must volunteer to participate and hope that the administration places a value on the contribution he has to offer.

As a team member, the school library media specialist contributes by

1. Advising of current trends and studies in curriculum design.
2. Advising the school staff on the use of media and instructional techniques to meet learning objectives.
3. Ensuring that a systematic approach to information skills instruction will be included in curriculum plans.
4. Recommending media and technologies appropriate to particular subject matter and activities.

Skill 4.2 Collaborative teaching and planning

The school library media specialist plays a vital role in curriculum design and directing the vision of a school. It is important for the library media specialist and the classroom teacher to form a strong collaborative partnership.

> **Learn more about collaborative planning**
>
> http://www.ncwiseowl.org/Impact/toolkit.htm

To support the **collaborative** process there are key skills the media specialist must possess. These include:

- Flexibility – have the ability to adjust to the differing needs of staff and students and flexibility with time

- Curriculum Expert – get to know the curriculum being taught at the grade levels being served. This makes the media specialist an invaluable partner.

- Leadership – set the path in which the media program should move toward, set goals and expectations, be the advocate for the teachers as well as the media program

- Approachable – establish good rapport with staff and students. Be someone they know will be willing to go above and beyond

- Persistence – keep going and keep the media program moving forward

Instructional planning for the school library media specialist is the process of effectively integrating library skills instruction into the curriculum.

Methods of instructional planning:

1. Identify content. Teachers create a list of instructional objectives for specific classes. Library media specialists, using state and local scope and sequence, prepare a list of objectives for teaching information skills.
2. Specify learning objectives. Teachers and library media specialists working together should merge the list of objectives
3. Examine available resources.
4. Determine instructional factors:
    a. Learner styles.
    b. Teaching techniques and teacher and library media specialists' division of responsibilities in the lesson implementation.
    c. Student groupings. Consider abilities, special needs, etc.
5. Pretest.
6. Determine activities to meet objectives.
7. Select specific resources and support agencies.
8. Implement the unit.
9. Evaluate.
10. Revise the objectives and/or activities.

To promote independent student learning the school library media specialist must work collaboratively with staff and students to teach information literacy skills. These tools are the stepping stones to self-directed and independent learning.

The school library media specialist plays an essential role by providing physical and intellectual access to resources. Through physical access patrons are able to locate a wide variety of resources quickly and easily. Special attention is paid to providing alternate formats to support student needs. By providing intellectual access to resources there is a wide array of topics to satisfy curiosity and to allow students to explore topics of interest.

Independence begins with a student questioning the world around them and being willing to seek answers. The school library media specialist can foster this through:
- Modeling the strategies that will teach students to be independent learners.
- Collaborating with teachers to develop effective strategies.
- Promoting the correct steps to take when working through an information literacy model.

Staff, including teachers and support personnel, should be offered periodic in-service in learning new skills and reinforcing known skills. These skills may be taught at formal, structured workshops or in informal small-group or individual sessions when a need arises.

1. A hands-on orientation for teachers new to school by the American Association of School Librarians to familiarize them with available resource and equipment and apprise them of services by the American Association of School Librarians should include information on incorporating appropriate media into their lessons. Written procedures for selection and evaluation should be available. Use a variety of media formats in presenting the information by the American Association of School Librarians overhead transparencies or LED projections for lists and forms; a videotape program on producing transparencies, slides, videotape, etc.; the automated card catalog for search procedures.
2. Provide information on new/existing media and solicit recommendations.
    a. Send bibliographies, catalogs, or newsletters frequently, asking for purchase suggestions.
    b. Inform all teachers of district and school preview policies and arrange previews for purchase suggestions.
    c. Involve as many teachers as possible on review committees.
3. Provide periodic brief refresher modules. Advertise the media and equipment to be used in each session. Suggest uses of each lesson's media format so teachers can make appropriate choices. Have teachers create one or more products at each session that can be used for instruction in an upcoming lesson.
4. Secure oral or written feedback on both teacher-made and commercial media used in classroom lessons. Ask them to use appropriate evaluation criteria in measuring the product's worth. The more familiar they become with the criteria, the better their product choices will become.

TEACHER CERTIFICATION STUDY GUIDE

Skill 4.3 **Knowledge of learning styles and developmental levels of students**

Bloom's Taxonomy is probably the most recognizable of all learning theories. Created by Benjamin Bloom, he reasons that there are various skill progressions.

1. Knowledge
Recall expects the ability to retell a story in proper sequence and to identify the characters and places where the events occur. School library media specialists can suggest titles of books, filmstrips or videotapes appropriate for each user's ability and interest. Young students can exhibit recall mastery by orally retelling the story, dramatizing the story through role play, and drawing pictures or making puppets of the characters. Mature students can develop a story board and create slides or videotapes of their own reenactment. PK-2 students should be expected to recall a list of instructions and act on them. Training them in the use of location, retrieval, and circulation procedures will enhance their listening skills so they can become productive media center users.

2. Comprehension.
Students in upper primary grades exhibit the ability to explain the main idea of a passage or the theme of a story. Reading, listening, and viewing can be enhanced by outlining the main points of a written passage, audiotape or record, and any of the visual media: filmstrips, slides, videotapes, and laser disks. At this level, they can produce slides, transparencies, posters, or models that demonstrate their understanding of the material. They can show the cause/effect relationship of happenings by discussing and practicing the behavioral procedures required to work cooperatively in the media center.

3. Application or Inference.
After reading a story/book, listening to a record or audiotape, or viewing a filmstrip or videotape, a middle school student should be able to interpret characters' actions, determine the logic of plot sequences, relate knowledge from the reading to real life, and infer information about characters from dialogue. They might predict a new course of action, were a given event to change. Some middle school and most high school students should be able to discuss inferences after reading, viewing, or listening to most media formats. Students at this point can learn to discriminate the appearance and function of various media formats and match them to appropriate learning activities. Students at this level may also be encouraged to study television production, photography or related media arts. Students may be planning and producing daily announcements via closed circuit television.

LIBRARY MEDIA

4. Analysis.
   Secondary students now judge the quality and appropriateness of reading materials, making selections independently. They can be expected to assess the quality of the author's writing style, the effectiveness of character and plot development, the bias of the writer's/producer's presentation, and the appropriateness of the language used to convey information. Students at this level should master concentrated listening skills by taking study notes from printed matter, lectures, or audiovisual programs. Learning should not only result in written research papers but in audiovisual projects. Students should be taught design, production, and editing skills.
5. Synthesis or Appreciation.
   Accomplishable in varying degrees at every level is the ability to express an emotional response to subject matter or a reaction to the author's language or a movie's theme or graphic detail. Younger students' reactions will be observable immediately. Requests for more of the same will keep the media specialist searching for similar materials. Older youngsters can be expected to write appraisals that incorporate evaluation and appreciation skills. Those with definite, vocal opinions may be encouraged to serve on the library media advisory committee.
6. Evaluation
   Make judgments about the value of ideas or materials.

Another learning theory includes Howard Gardner's **Multiple Intelligences**.

> **Learn more about multiple intelligences**
>
> http://www.howardgardner.com/MI/mi.html

- Visual/Spatial Intelligence
  These learners tend to think in pictures. They enjoy looking at maps, charts, pictures, videos, and movies.
- Verbal/Linguistic Intelligence
  These learners have good auditory skills and are generally elegant speakers. They think in words rather than pictures.
- Logical/Mathematical Intelligence
  These learners think conceptually in logical and numerical patterns making connections between pieces of information.
- Bodily/Kinesthetic Intelligence
  These learners express themselves through movement.
- Musical/Rhythmic Intelligence
  These musically inclined learners think in sounds, rhythms and patterns.
- Interpersonal Intelligence
  These learners try to see things from other people's point of view in order to understand how they think and feel.
- Intrapersonal Intelligence
  These learners try to understand their inner feelings, dreams, relationships with others, and strengths and weaknesses.

- Naturalist Intelligence
  These learners focus upon nature and the environment.

Skill 4.4　Knowledge of teaching and assessment strategies

Despite the diversity of responsibilities, a school library media specialist is first and foremost a teacher. The percentage of time devoted to structured teaching activities is greater in elementary school, especially if the media center is still on rigid scheduling. As students mature, structured lessons should be shortened and followed by longer hands-on activities for reinforcement of the learned skills.

Several factors have contributed to defining the school library media specialist's instructional role.
1. Introduction of pre-kindergarten programs into elementary schools. As more public schools have introduced PK programs, many states have expanded certification parameters. However, training in understanding that age group and its unique needs has not kept pace. One survey indicated that most certified media specialists considered parenthood their best qualification for dealing with preschoolers.
2. Greater emphasis on developing higher order thinking skills. Even in primary grades, students are encouraged to synthesize information and make media productions to present the results of their learning. Middle school students should be reading critically and making value judgments about the quality of their reading material.
3. Cooperative planning and learning. Research affirms that information skills instruction must be integrated into the curriculum. Furthermore, the days of silence in libraries has given way to learning noise, students working in groups with the necessary communication. Working in teams gives the students preparation for the real work world.

At all levels, library media specialists should be expected to
1. Train students in information location using traditional and new information retrieval skills.
2. Facilitate students' understanding of different media formats and the purpose of various information presentation formats.
3. Assist students in developing critical thinking skills in relation to the located information.
4. Reinforce library media citizenship skills.
5. Teach information skills.

Assessment:
1. Students' reading habits can be evaluated by use of student surveys or interviews, by packaged assessment programs like Accelerated Reader, or by some in-house record keeping system. Several good standardized tests exist for testing reading progress.
2. Visual literacy can be evaluated by observing students' own visual designs, from drawings, graphic designs, and photographs to motion pictures and computer graphics. Students must also be able to verbally analyze various images they perceive and to interpret messages delivered.
3. Listening skills are evaluated by observing the student's ability to follow oral directions, to remember facts and details, and to retell a series of pieces of information. Standardized or teacher-made tests can pre-test and post-test listening skills mastery.
4. Media literacy is evaluated by observing students' use of equipment needed to create productions and noting the final product of media projects for appropriateness of format, length and depth of coverage, graphic quality, focus, and the like.

Skill 4.5   Orientation techniques

Providing an orientation program is essential to the success of the school library media center. Areas of orientation should include sessions for students, school staff, volunteers, and parents or community members.

Students

When introducing students to the media center and its programs, it is important to teach them the following:
- location of resources
- procedures for checking in and out resources
- skills needed to find resources
- information regarding any special programs the media center offers either during school or after hours
- skills of how to access resources at home our outside of school

These orientation sessions could take place during a class period or during special after hour programs.

The main point of the orientation should be to provide students with the information they need to maximize their use of the school library media center and its resources.

In order to provide more effective student access, teachers and school **staff** need to be more aware of what the media center has to offer. One of the best things a school library media specialist can do is to meet with the teachers and share not only the information provided to the students, but how they can be a valuable resource for the classroom teacher.

Collaborative planning sessions with the teachers allow the school library media specialist to meet one-on-one or with small groups of teachers to share teaching strategies, resources, and programs that may enhance teaching units.

One tool that is imperative to the success of the school library media program is to have a designated time during faculty meetings to provide a library media update. In just a five minute time teachers can receive an update on new resources and upcoming events as well as where to go to receive additional information.

To make effective use of media **volunteers** they will need to become acclimated to the workings of the media center. Before they perform their specific task it is imperative that they receive training on proper procedures. Techniques can include observation and formal training sessions.

Parents and community members can become better involved in the learning process when they are informed. Open House times and parent nights provide prime opportunities to share information regarding the resources the media center offers. Special events such as family reading nights or technology nights can showcase specific resources. When conducting special events, it is important to utilize student volunteers. When the students are involved, the parents will be as well.

Skill 4.6   Knowledge of information literacy models and principles

Information literacy can be defined as the capability to understand when information is needed and to identify, evaluate, and use the information effectively. It combines what we've known for years with the skills needed to thrive in the future. With the increased access to information that is possible because of technology, it is crucial for learners to not only be able to locate information but to distinguish between that which is valid and that which is not.

Learn more about the Big6 Model
http://www.big6.com/

There are many information literacy models. One of the most commonly used is the **Big6** model. It was created by educators Mike Eisenberg and Bob Berkowitz. The Big6 process outlines how people solve an information problem. They have broken down this process into six stages.

1. **Task Definition** – identify problem and information needed
2. **Information Seeking Strategies** – decide on sources of information and select the best
3. **Location and Access** – locate the sources and search for the information
4. **Use of Information** – interact with the information and pick out that which is most relevant
5. **Synthesis** – organize the information and present it
6. **Evaluation** – evaluate its effectiveness of the product and the process

Another popular model includes the Pathways to Knowledge Information Skills Model. It was created by Professor Marjorie Pappas and Follett Software's Director of Curriculum Ann Tepe. This model outlines strategies that include appreciation, pre-search, search, interpretation, communication, and evaluation.

Skill 4.7   Teaching use of information resources and search strategies

As students begin to search for information resources for research or other projects, it is important to evaluate the resources selected for their effectiveness.

There are several key factors to consider when looking at any type of resource be it a book or web page.

These criteria include the following:

1. Audience: Who was this information intended to reach? What is the level of the information?

2. Scope: How detailed is the information? Is this work focused on an overall outline of the topic or does it provide in depth information on one specific aspect of the topic?

3. When was the information published? How often is the website updated?

4. Who is the author? What authority does this person have to be writing this article?

5. Is the article free from bias? Is it from a single person or an organization trying to argue for a certain position?

6. Does the author include their resource bibliography?

7. Does the information come from a scholarly article/magazine or from a popular article/magazine?

Whether searching for information in print indices or electronic resources, it is necessary to formulate strategies for locating information prior to beginning a search to save time and effort.

Write down words or phrases that directly relate to the topic being covered. Start with general terms and then break them down into more specific areas. These terms become the keywords that will be used in the search. A keyword is an important word or phrase that is used to retrieve information.

Once the keyword(s) has been determined, use it to search books, articles, or electronic resources. When searching through print materials the researcher will look for specific subject headings. Subject headings are words or phrases that are used to locate resources by topics.

When information can be found under more than one subject heading the information is often cross-referenced. The words "See also" may be used to direct the researcher to a more appropriate heading.

Electronic resources offer a wider array of strategies for locating information. Two of the most common strategies can be explained as follows:

- Boolean operators: Popular operators include: AND, AND NOT, and OR. These are used to narrow keyword searches.

- Wildcards: This is an effective tool if one is unsure of the spelling or date for the topic being searched. An example would include the search for a list of all names in a database beginning with the letters ph. One way to phrase the search is to type PH* The asterisk at the end will cause the search to return anything in the database that begins with the letters "PH."

When conducting a search it may be necessary to modify search strategies or parameters in order to narrow the results or to find more relevant information. One of the first places to begin is by analyzing the results that have been returned. Are their certain references that you do not want that continuously appear in the search? Is the specific topic appearing?

Three categories of results seem to appear. The user will receive too many records, too few records, or no relevant records.

hen too many records are returned, the user may need to narrow their topic or make it more specific. Using Boolean strategies to eliminate unnecessary returns can make a difference. Another strategy would be to put key phrases in quotation marks so that the terms would be listed together.

When a search returns too few records, it may be necessary to broaden the search. The topic may have been too narrow. Take a look at any relevant records that were returned and evaluate the descriptors to locate potential terms to add to the search.

If no relevant records are returned, check the spelling of the search topic or look for the information in a different source.

The World Wide Web has brought information directly to the end-user. With such an abundance of information, it is important to teach students and adults how to discriminate the good from the bad. When looking at online information there are key points to consider.

1. How accurate is the information?
2. Who wrote the information? What authority do they have on the subject?
3. What type of site is it? Commercial is .com, organizational is .org, educational is .edu, government is .gov, television is .tv, and so on.
4. How current is the information?
5. Is it easy to navigate or does it require special software to load?

TEACHER CERTIFICATION STUDY GUIDE

COMPETENCY 5.0 PROFESSIONAL DEVELOPMENT, LEADERSHIP, AND ADVOCACY

Skill 5.1 Professional development, such as continuing education programs

Designing a **staff development** activity follows a basic lesson profile with special considerations for adult learners.

1. Analyze learner styles. Adult learners are more receptive to role playing and individual performance before a group. Learner motivation is more internal, but some external motivations, such as release time, compensatory time, in service credit or some written recognition, might be discussed with the principal.
2. Assess learner needs. Survey teachers to determine which media or equipment they want to learn more about. Consider environmental factors: time, place, and temperature. Since many in service activities occur after school, taking the lesson to the teachers in their own classrooms may make them more comfortable, especially if they can have a reviving afternoon snack. If they must come to the media center, serve refreshments.
3. Select performance objectives. Determine exactly what the teacher should be able to do at the end of a successful in service session.

4. Plan activities to achieve objectives. Demonstrate the skill to be taught, involve the participants in active performance/production, and allow for practice and feedback.
5. Select appropriate resources. Arrange that all materials and equipment are ready and in good functioning order on the day of the in service.
6. Determine instructor. Either the school library media specialist or a faculty member should conduct these on-site in services unless the complexity or novelty of the technology requires an outside expert.
7. Provide continuing support. The instructor or designated substitute should be available after the in service for reinforcement.
8. Evaluation. Determine the effectiveness of the in service and make modifications as recommended in future in services.

Because we are in the business of teaching, all technologies must be viewed as educational tools. To enable teachers to understand the way these technologies can be applied in their classrooms, they must understand the relationship between these tools and learning needs. The school library media professionals must be able to update teachers on this correlation.

1. Conduct timely, short in-service activities to demonstrate and allow teachers to manipulate new technologies and plan classroom uses
2. Clip articles or write reviews to distribute to teachers with suggestions for application in their particular learning environment.
3. Offer to plan and teach lessons in different content areas.

Skill 5.2 Awareness of the role and function of professional organizations, such as ALA, AASL, and AECT

National guidelines for school library media programs are provided in documents published by the American Association of School Librarians (AASL), a division of the American Library Association (ALA), and the Association for Educational Communications and Technology (AECT).

Information Power: Guidelines for School Library Media Programs a collaboration of AASL/AECT, was published in 1988 to provide standardized national guidelines as a vision for school library media programs into the 21st century. The AASL/AECT Standards Writing Committee and contributors from public school districts and universities across the country, using standards that have been revised over the last thirty years, created a definitive work.

These revised standards reflect the flexibility to manage today's library media centers and to direct centers into the future. The AASL/AECT mission objectives were echoed in President Bush's message during a speech at the 1991 White House Conference on Library and Information Services. The following is a summary of the guidelines culled from these and other publications:

1. A democratic society guarantees the right of its populace to be well-informed. To this end, libraries and media centers of all kinds are the bastions of intellectual freedom.
2. Literacy for all United States residents begins in the public school system. School readiness through access to ample media stimuli, facilities that provide physical access to materials across cultural and economic barriers, and a sound national goal, supported by legislative funding, will ensure that Americans can avail themselves of the information to which they are entitled.
3. Americans will become more productive in the workplace by taking advantage of the technology offered in the Information Age. To support the school-to-work initiative, school library media centers must offer access and instruction in emerging technologies used in business and industry.
4. Collaborative efforts between schools, business, and community agencies will encourage life-long learning. *Information Power's* mission statement and the vision statements of many public schools specify life-long learning as their primary objective. Thus libraries, even in the schools, must become community centers, offering their materials and services to all segments of the public. Such open access also motivates school-aged students as they see adults continually seeking information and educational opportunities.

In the list of resources at the end of this guide are many titles that provide information on school library media programs. *Information Power* (AASL/AECT), *Taxonomies of the School Library Media Program* (Loertscher), and *Administering the School Library Media Center* (Gillespie and Spirt) are three of the best-known and most accessible.

Less accessible but a valuable reference tool is the six-volume set titled *School Library Media Annual* (Smith, Aaron, and Scales, Eds.), each volume dealing with different aspects of school library media programs.

Among periodicals *The School Library Media Quarterly* (AASL) offers scholarly articles that are research based. *Media and Methods* presents information on integrating media into the curriculum. *Tech Trends* (AECT) examines the impact of technology and innovations in media use.

Skill 5.3 **Familiarity with professional resources, such as professional journals, library literature, and *Information Power***

Professional development resources are extensive in scope as evidenced by the resource list in this guide.

Other sources include the college and university programs offered at many state and private institutions. Degrees in library science, information science, or educational media are offered for both undergraduates and graduate students. Some universities offer extern programs or on-line courses.

Workshops are offered at state conferences and through district in-service programs.

Library Media Organizations

National:
American Association of School Library (AASL)
American Library Association
50 East Huron Street
Chicago IL 60611

Association for Educational Communications and Technology (AECT)
1126 Sixteenth Street, NW
Washington DC 20036

Related Organizations

National:

National Education Association (NEA)
1201 North Street NW
Washington DC 20036-3290

American Federation of Teachers (AFT)
555 New Jersey Avenue, NW
Washington DC 20001-2079

Phi Delta Kappa International, Inc.
408 N. Union
P. O. Box 789
Bloomington IN 47402

International Reading Association
800 Barksdale Road
Newark DE 19711-3269

Association of Supervision and Curriculum Development (ASCD)
1250 N. Pitt Street
Alexandria VA 22314-1453

Skill 5.4   Community involvement

By connecting with the community the school library media specialist can expand the resources available to students and strengthen community support of the school and the media program.

There are three main areas in which a school library media specialist can best provide community support and in turn have the community involved in the learning program.

Collaboration
It is crucial to develop strong relationships with families, public agencies, colleges, universities, and government agencies. Strong relationships with families can encourage a child's learning. These family members may in turn become volunteers for the media program. When school libraries cooperate with public agencies, the school library media specialist builds valuable links to resources, potential funding and long-term community commitment. Colleges and universities supply professional knowledge to the media specialist as well as research that enhances best teaching practices. Finally, collaboration with government agencies and professional organizations allows the school library media specialist to participate in shaping the future.

Leadership
It is important to provide programs for the adults in the community. By providing after-hour access to school resources the school library media specialist can become a community learning center. Mentoring and tutoring programs can provide opportunities for both adults and students to participate in community projects.

Technology
Technology allows people to keep in constant contact. The school library media specialist can increase the global impact of the media program. Web services allow parents to stay in touch with happenings at school. Distance learning experiences can expand the opportunities students have available. The use of technology in general can bring the world to students. They are no longer limited by physical boundaries.

Skill 5.5 Codes of ethics

All libraries have certain guidelines that should be followed. The American Library Association has created a Library Bill of Rights, while the Association of Educational Communications and Technology has designed a **Code of Ethics**.

> **Learn more about AECT's Code of Ethics**
>
> http://www.aect.org/About/Ethics.asp

The Library Bill of Rights agrees that libraries are places to obtain information and develop ideas. A brief description of each policy is as follows:
- resources should include a representation of all ideas, concepts and background
- resources should not be excluded because of the viewpoint or concept
- censorship of information should be challenged
- a person should not be denied access to a library for any reason
- libraries are a public space and should be available for use to all

AECT's Code of Ethics includes a preamble and three sections. Section one outlines the commitment to the individual. Section two addresses the commitment to society. Section three discusses the commitment to the profession.

The Preamble provides a description of the code of ethics. Section one explains that a library should encourage independent learning, protect individual rights, promote professional development with regards to technology, should provide and educational program that develops the learner, and follow the first amendment. The second section, Commitment to Society, outlines that a member shall honestly represent their organization, should not accept gifts of favors that would impair their judgment as a professional, and shall follow fair and equitable practices. The final section, Commitment to the Profession, describes that members should treat all other members fairly, should not exploit their membership for monetary gain, shall abide by and educate others in copyright law, and shall observe all laws that relate to their profession.

Libraries of all kinds face the issue of censorship. The American Library Association began to print the journal, *The Newsletter of Intellectual Freedom*, to keep librarians informed of current cases regarding censorship.

The National Council of Teachers of English (NCTE) developed **"The Right to Read" statement**. In summary, the statement outlines the fact that everyone has the right to read information on any topic they choose.

> **Learn more about NCTE's "The Right to Read" statement**
>
> http://www.ncte.org/about/over/positions/level/gen/107616.htm

Skill 5.6 Awareness of issues and trends

To stay ahead of the curve, school library media specialist must stay abreast of the latest **trends and issues** regarding librarianship. The American Library Association is an excellent resource for such information. Topics include:

• Flexible vs. fixed scheduling—how to make the transformation

• Collaboration—To maximize student learning, collaboration between school library media specialists and teachers is crucial. Effective techniques can develop authentic learning experiences.

> **Learn more about current issues and trends**
>
> http://www.ala.org/ala/aasl/aaslissues/issuesadvocacy.cfm

• New online information resources and instructional technologies—assist with the location of information and operation of new technologies

• Evaluating information—As a result of the technological boom there has been a flood of information available. Learning to discriminate between relevant and irrelevant information is essential for students

• The evolution of instructional materials—The use of paper as we know it in the classroom will slowly give way to information in a digital format. Electronic books and magazines online are just a few of the formats now available.

• Media center design for the digital age—Planning for distance learning opportunities and technology instruction, considerations for learning outside of the normal school days

• Promoting the media program

• Continuing professional development and certification requirements

• Interlibrary loan

• Changes in children's literature

Skill 5.7 Advocacy

Building support for the school library media program creates a network of individuals willing to work to enhance the learning experiences for students. It all begins with a program mission that supports advocacy.

The American Library Association has developed an Advocacy Toolkit to assist libraries in promoting their programs. Parts of this toolkit include:

- **@ Your Library program**—outlines the role of the school library media specialist and the programs they manage
- There are PowerPoint presentations that explain **@ Your Library** and provide topics of discussion
- Implementation plan for Information Power
- Brochures for promoting advocacy
- Guides for meeting with government officials
- Resource guides for promoting the media center, intellectual freedom and other topics
- Communication handbook

> **Learn more about @ Your Library**
> http://www.ala.org/ala/proftools/21centurylit/21stcenturyliteracy.htm

Skill 5.8 Certification and accreditation

Certification requirements differ by state. Some states only require a school library media specialist to have a special license or certification while others require a Master's degree. It is best to contact the state department of education where one plans to work to inquire about certification. Many states will accept certification from other states.

One option open to currently certified school library media specialists it to pursue **National Board Certification** in Library Media. To be eligible for national board certification one must have been teaching for three years, hold a bachelor's degree and have a valid teaching license. Obtaining National Board Certification is one of the highest symbols of educational achievement.

> **Learn more about National Board Certification**
> http://www.nbpts.org/the_standards/standards_by_cert?ID=19&x=47&y=13

Another means of receiving certification and accreditation is through the Southern Association of Colleges and Schools. It provides accreditation guidelines for K-12 schools including recommendations for school library media centers. For instance, a school with 500-749 students should have one full time media specialist and four support staff for administration, media or technology.

TEACHER CERTIFICATION STUDY GUIDE

Other information includes:
- minimum of ten books per student
- maintaining a comprehensive collection of resources
- has a circulation system
- ensures that staff collaborate to provide enhanced learning experiences for students
- provides professional development
- budget is adequate for support of the school library media program
- has Acceptable Use Internet policy

Skill 5.9 Legislation affecting libraries and education, such as laws on intellectual freedom and equal access, and the Children's Internet Protection Act

National:

1965 Elementary and Secondary Education Act Title III – This legislation impacted school libraries by encouraging their expansion into media centers.

1981 Education Consolidation and Improvement Act – Chapter II of this bill included regulations and funding in the form of block grants for school library media resources and instructional equipment. Funding ended with the 1994-95 school year.

> Learn more about court cases and legislation affecting education
>
> http://www.ala.org/ala/issues/issuesadvocacy.htm

1995 Innovative Educational Programs Legislation – This three-year program provides block grants for innovative uses of technology in schools, including library media centers.

The principles of intellectual freedom are guaranteed by the First Amendment to the Constitution of the United States. They are reinforced in the Library Bill of Rights adapted by the ALA in 1948, the AECT's statement on intellectual freedom (1978), the freedom to read and review statements of the ALA (1953 and 1979), and the National Council of English Teachers, Students Right to Read Statement.

The principles as they relate to children:

1. Freedom of access to information in all formats through activities that develop critical thinking and problem solving skills.
2. Freedom of access to ideas that present a variety of points of view through activities that teach discriminating reading.
3. Freedom to acquire information reflective of the intellectual, physical, and social growth of the user.

LIBRARY MEDIA

It becomes the responsibility of the school library media specialist to develop and maintain a collection development policy (4.6.1) that ensures these freedoms.

Despite the best collection development policies, an occasional complaint will arise. In our society the following issues cause controversy: politics, gay rights, profanity, pornography, creationism vs. evolution, the occult, sex education, racism and violence. Adults disagree philosophically about these issues. They will often express their concern first to the school library media specialist.

Ethically, he is bound to protect the principles of intellectual freedom, but he is also bound by those same principles to treat the complaint seriously as the expression of an opposing view.

The most important thing is not to panic. The challenge is not an affront to the media specialist but a complaint about the content, language, or graphics in a material. The first step is to greet the complainant calmly and explain the principles of intellectual freedom you are bound to uphold. A good paraphrase from the AECT Statement is that a learner's right to access information can only be abridged by an agreement between parent and child. With the current emphasis on the V chip for selective television viewing, parents are becoming more aware of their own roles in censoring unwanted images from their children.

Judicial rulings have come in the area of copyright issues. The 1975 ruling in the case of *Williams & Wilkins Co. v. U.S.* provided guidance to legislators in preparing the fair use provisions of the 1976 Copyright Act.

It ruled that entire articles may be mass-duplicated for use that advances the public welfare without doing economic harm to the publishers. This ruling provides encouragement to educators that fair use may be interpreted more liberally.

In 1984, the ruling in *Sony Corp. of America v. Universal City Studios, Inc.* placed the burden of proving infringement on the plaintiff. The Supreme Court upheld the right of individuals to off-air videotape television programs for non-commercial use. Thus, a copyright holder must prove that the use of videotaped programming is intentionally harmful. Civil suits against educators would require the plaintiff to prove that the existing or potential market would be negatively affected by use of these programs in a classroom setting.

Current fair use practice specifies that a videotaped copy must be shown within 10 days of its airing and be kept no longer than 45 days for use in constructing supplemental teaching materials related to the programming.

Court rulings have ambiguously addressed the issue of censorship. In 1972, the U.S. Court of Appeals for the Second Circuit (*President's Council v. Community School Board No. 25, New York City*) ruled in favor of the removal of a library book, reasoning that its removal did not oppose or aid religion.

In 1976, the Court of Appeals for the Sixth Circuit (*Minarcini v. Strongsville City School District*) ruled against the removal of Joseph Heller's *Catch 22* and two Kurt Vonnequt novels on the grounds that removal of books from a school library is a burden on the freedom of classroom discussion and an infringement of the First Amendment's guarantee of an individual's "right to know."

A Massachusetts district court (*Right to Read Defense Committee v. School Board of the City of Chelsea*) ordered the school board to return to the high school library a poetry anthology that contained "objectionable and filthy" language. The court asserted that the school had control over curriculum but not library collections.

Three cases in the 1980s dealt with challenging the removal of materials from high school libraries. The first two, in circuit courts, condemned the burning of banned books (*Zykan v. Warsaw Community School Corporation, Indiana*) and the removal of books of considerable literary merit. The case of *Board of Education, Island Trees Union Free School District 26 (New York) v. Pico* reached the Supreme Court in 1982 after the U.S. Court of Appeals for the Second Circuit had reversed a lower court ruling granting the school board the right to remove nine books that had been deemed "anti-American, anti-Semitic, anti-Christian and just plain filthy." The Supreme Court in a 5-4 ruling upheld the Court of Appeals' ruling and the nine books were returned. The dissenting opinion, however, continued to foster ambiguity claiming that, if the intent was to deny free access to ideas, it was an infringement of the First Amendment, but if the intent was to remove pervasively vulgar material, the board had just cause. Ultimately, the issue hinged on a school board's authority in determining the selection of optional rather than required reading. Library books, being optional, should not be denied to users.

In most instances, a calm, rational discussion will satisfy the challenger.

However, if the challenge is pursued, the media specialist will have to follow district procedures for handling the complaint. The appropriate school administrator should be informed. Of course, an administrator may have been confronted initially. In either instance, the complainant is asked to fill out a formal complaint form, citing his specific objection in a logical manner. Sometimes, simply thinking the issue through clearly and recognizing that someone will truly listen to his complaint is enough of a solution. If all else fails, a reconsideration committee should be appointed to take the matter under advisement and recommend a course of action.

RESOURCES

1. American Association of School Librarians (AASL) and Association for Educational Communications and Technology (AECT). *Information Power: Building Partnerships for Learning.* Chicago: American Library Association and Association for Educational Communications and Technology, 1998.

   A sourcebook for presenting professional guidelines for developing school library media programs into the twenty-first century. It includes chapters on establishing and maintaining a school library media program; defining the role of the school library media professional and paraprofessional personnel; determining the resources, equipment, and facilities necessary to meet the goals; and spelling out leadership responsibilities of district, region, and state. Appendices contain policy statements of different organizations, present research results, and provide budget formulas and minimum standards for facilities spaces.

2. American Library Association, Canadian Library Association, and The Library Association. *Anglo-American Cataloging Rules.* 2nd ed. Chicago: American Library Association, 2005.

   A revised edition that provides rules for including technology changes.

3. American Library Association, Office for Intellectual Freedom Staff. *Intellectual Freedom Manual.* 7th ed. Chicago: American Library Association, 2005.

   Updated in 2005, this manual presents the statements of rights of various library organizations, provides the ALA Intellectual Freedom statement and its implications for library media programs, discusses laws and court cases, advises on methods to deal with censorship, and presents promotion techniques.

4. Anderson, Pauline H. *Planning School Library Media Facilities.* Hamden, CT: The Shoe String Press, 1990.

   This extensive work traces the creation of a school library media center from politicking to moving in. Much emphasis is placed on the planning process. Five specific case studies are offered to show how the process works.

5. Baker, D. Philip. *The Library Media Program and the School.* Englewood, CO: Libraries Unlimited, 1984.

   A thorough discussion of the school library media program in relation to the total school mission and objectives.

6. Bannister, Barbara Farley, Janice B. Carlile, and Kathy Baron. *Elementary School Librarian's Survival Guide: Ready-to-Use Tips, Techniques, and Materials to Help You Save Time and Work in Virtually Every Aspect.* NY: The Center for Applied Research in Education, 1993.

   A great guide for either setting up a new media center or operating an existing one. It deals with the physical management of the media center; successful discipline; reading promotions; special programs; story times, book talks, and library skills; building support with the school community; budgeting; selection procedures; new technologies; inventory and weeding; and avoiding burnout. Full of practical suggestions and reproducibles.

7. Brown, J.W.; R.B. Lewis; and F.F. Harcleroad. *AV Instruction: Technology, Media, and Methods.* 6th ed. New York: McGraw-Hill, 1983.

   A good reference book on the use of instructional materials and technology at all educational levels. It provides information on planning instruction, using and producing various media, operating audiovisual equipment, and designing facilities for using media. It also provides information on copyright laws.

8. Buchanan, Jan. *Flexible Access Library Media Programs.* Englewood, CO: Libraries Unlimited, 1991.

   A fine reference tool for understanding and developing approaches to designing flexible access programs for school library media centers. Presents an overview of current research on integrating the teaching of library skills into the curriculum, a whole language approach to teaching reading, and the importance of encouraging critical thinking. The book's greatest value is showing the building level media specialist the techniques for involving the total school community in the planning and implementation of integrated lessons and defining the roles of all the participants involved in the planning, execution and evaluation stages. Emphasis is on the cooperative planning required and on the measurable benefit to the learner.

9. Bucher, Katherine T. *Computers & Technology in School Library Media Centers*. Columbus, OH: Linworth Publishing, 1994.

   This 3-ring bound publication offers a thorough discussion of technology's relevance to libraries. It includes as contents (1) working with instructional technology in the 1990s, (2) computer basics, (3) library management with a computer, (4) multimedia CD-ROM, (5) videodisks in the library. Out of print but may be available in a library.

10. Carlsen, G. Robert. *Books and the Teenage Reader: A Guide for Parents, Teachers and Librarians*. New York: Harper and Row, 1980.

    This ageless work discusses teenage interests and social/personal needs and provides reading lists in different genres, interest areas, classics, etc.

11. Gillespie, John and Catherine Barr. *Best Books for Middle School and Junior High Readers*. Englewood, CO: Libraries Unlimited, 2004.

    A reference guide to selecting titles for middle school readers. Presents examples of literature within certain genres, discusses themes appropriate to middle grade readers based on personal, social, and academic needs.

12. Hagler, Ronald. *The Bibliographic Record and Information Technology*. 3rd ed. Chicago: American Library Association, 1997.

    A serious, detailed study of cataloging, bibliographic standards and controls using MARC record format.

13. Hannigan, J.A. and Glenn Estes. *Media Center Facilities Design*. Chicago: American Library Association, 1978.

    Expanding on the ALA discussion of facilities design in the original *Information Power,* these authors have presented methods and models for media facilities for all school levels, discussing factors for planning, design, and construction, even offering architectural renderings.

14. Hart, Thomas. *The School Library Media Facilities Planner (Best Practices for School Library Media)*. NY: Neal-Schuman Publishers 2006.

    Drawing on Hart's 30 years experience as a library consultant, this book tells how to design, build, remodel, and equip a school library media center.

15. Haycock, Ken, Barbara Edwards, Michelle Dober. *The Neal-Schuman Authoritative Guide to Kids' Search Engines, Subject Directories, and Portals.* NY: Neal-Schuman, 2003.

    Includes descriptions of search engines and checklists for evaluating them.

16. Helm, V. M. *What Educators Should Know About Copyright.* Phi Delta Kappa Educational Foundation, 1986.

    A brief, but thorough, discussion of copyright law, the court cases that have tested that law, and the implications of the rulings on schools, including library media programs.

17. Huck, Charlotte S. et al. *Children's Literature in the Elementary School.* 8th ed. NY: McGraw-Hill, 2003.

    Includes student CD and Litlinks Activity Books. Both a textbook in child development and the literature designed to meet children's needs, a study of genres, and a presentation of methods for teaching children's literature. Lists of book awards, authors, illustrators, periodicals, and publishers .

18. Intner, Sheila S. *Circulation Policy in Academic, Public, and School Libraries.* New York: Greenwood Press, 1987.

    This book deals with circulation policies in academic, public, and school libraries. Specific circulation plans from schools around the country offer models.

19. Intner, Sheila S. and Jean Weihs. *Standard Cataloging for School and Public Libraries.* 4th ed. Englewood, CO: Libraries Unlimited, 2007.

    Written for public librarians and school library media specialists, this book explains the principles and standards of cataloging. A thorough discussion of AACR rules, descriptions, subject headings, classification systems, and the like, but avoids arcane details that are most likely not encountered by the intended audience.

20. Katz, William A. *Introduction to Reference Work.* (Vol. 1) Basic Information Services. 8th ed. NY: McGraw-Hill, 2002.

    A study of traditional basic reference sources and methods for using these sources to answer reference questions. Includes an overview of the reference process and on-line reference services and their applications.

21. Kemp, Jerrold. *Planning, Producing, and Using Instructional Media.* 7th ed. Boston: Allyn & Bacon, 1993.

    Practical guide to media production techniques and methods of instruction. Summarizes research on the effectiveness of instructional materials and explains the method of developing an instructional program.

22. Kinney, Lisa F. *Lobby for Your Library: Know What Works.* Chicago, IL: American Library Association, 1992.

    Chapter 8 deals specifically with lobbying for schools, presenting typical funding sources and offering strategies to be used by key participants in lobbying agencies from local to state.

23. Klasing, Jane P. *Designing and Renovating School Library Media Centers.* Chicago: American Library Association, 1991.

    A quick reference for use by school personnel in planning and implementing an efficient facilities design. Sample floor plans and appendices full of bid forms, architectural symbols, and furniture details simplify the process.

24. Lance, Keith C. *The Impact of School Library Media Centers on Academic Achievement.* Castle Rock, CO: Hi Willow Research and Publishing, 1997.

    A research-based discussion of factors of library media programs that have directly influenced the improvement in student grades, standardized scores, and self-directed learning.

25. Laughlin, Mildred K. and Kathy H. Latrobe. (Eds.) *Public Relations for School Library Media Centers.* Englewood, CO: Libraries Unlimited, 1990.

    Seventeen articles about different facets of promoting the school library media program, including definitions of public relations, the library media specialist's attitude and interpersonal skills, stress and public relations, and specific groups to motivate.

26. Loertscher, David V. *Taxonomies of the School Library Media Program.* 2nd ed. Columbus, OH: Linworth Publishing, 200.

    One of the most outstanding works on elements of the school library media center program. Outlines the roles of media professionals, students, teachers, and administrators in integrating the library media program into the school curriculum. Models for personnel and program evaluation are included in appendices.

27. Morris, Betty J. *Administering the School Library Media Center.* 4th edition. Englewood, CO: Libraries Unlimited, 2004.

    A guide to practical considerations in operating a school library media center. Chapters on acquisition, organization, and management, with chapters on new technologies. Presents example of a policies and procedures manual. Revised in 1993.

28. Nilsen, Alleen and Kenneth Donelson. *Literature for Today's Young Adults.* 8th ed. Boston: Allyn & Bacon, 2008.

    A textbook dealing with print media: the history and trends of young adult literature; genres of special interest; using materials with young adults; and guidelines for evaluating these works. Presents brief statements about works of both recognized merit and potential interest to young adults and sketches of authors known in the field.

29. Pillon, N. B. *Reaching Young People Through Media.* Englewood, CO: Libraries Unlimited, 1983.

    Fifteen articles dealing with such topics as reading interests, materials selection, genres, censorship, youth advocacy, and technology.

30. Prostano, Emanuel T. and Joyce S. Prostano. *The School Library Media Center.* 3rd ed. Englewood, CO: Libraries Unlimited, 1999.

    Revised in 1999, this book deals with the library media center program development, administration and evaluation. There are also chapters on curriculum integration, media personnel, facilities and furniture, media and equipment, and the budget.

31. Reichman, Henry. *Censorship and Selection: Issues and Answers for Schools.* Chicago: American Library Association, 2001.

    This book addresses the specific problems of intellectual freedom encountered in schools. It discusses issues that are in dispute, selection policies and the law. It also offers possible solutions to complaints.

32. Report from the White House Office of the Press Secretary on the 1991 White House Conference on Library and Information Services. *Florida Media Quarterly* (Spring 1992), 16-17.

    An article summarizing President Bush's comments resulting from the conference in which he pledges executive support for full literacy by the year 2000.

33. Matthews, Joseph. *Strategic Planning and Management for Library Managers*. Englewood, CO: Libraries Unlimited, 2005.

    A comprehensive guide for planning for all types of libraries, especially useful in discussing leadership, organization, and evaluation techniques. Especially effective in defining mission statement and distinguishing between goals and objectives.

34. *School Library Media Annual.* Shirley Aaron and Pat Scales (Eds.) [1983-1987 Eds.] and Jane Bandy Smith (Ed.) [1988-1997 Eds.]. Englewood, CO: Libraries Unlimited.

    Each volume contains articles on national and state legislation, professional organizations, government affairs, and publications of note. Individual volumes highlight special issues.

    Volume 1: adolescent development, intellectual freedom, certification, instructional radio and television, software evaluations, networking.

    Volume 2: lobbying, continuing education, declining enrollment, impact of library media programs on student achievement, telecommunications.

    Volume 3: censorship; intellectual freedom committees, copyright concerns, interactive video, microcomputers in schools, ethical considerations.

    Volume 4: professionalizing the media profession; planning effective programs; information skills; facilities design; intellectual freedom, censorship, and copyright; managing on-line services.

    Volume 5: copyright for new technologies; selection policies and procedures; continuing education; leadership skills; advisory committees; promoting information and inquiry skills.

    Volume 6: whole language impact on media, censorship, research on library media centers, updates on automation.

    Volume 7: measuring services, developing standards, personnel, flexible scheduling, accreditation, state guidelines, implementing *Information Power*, partnership of NCATE and ALA/AASL.

    Volume 8: instructional consulting role, principal's role in creating vision for school library media programs, learning styles, designing effective instruction, contributions of technology, information literacy.

35. *The School Library Program in the Curriculum*. Englewood, CO: Libraries Unlimited, 1990.

    This collection of essays/opinion papers by Haycock and others deals with the media center in the context of the total school, the role of the teacher librarian, program planning and development, integrating information skills across the curriculum, secondary school applications, and issues and concerns.

36. Smaldino, Sharon et. al. *Instructional Technology and Media for Learning & Clips from the Classroom Package. 8th ed.* NY: Prentice Hall, 2005.

    Describes current and future technologies applied in classroom instruction and includes video to illustrate effective uses of technology.

37. Smith, Jane B. *Library Media Center Programs for Middle Schools: A Curriculum-Based Approach*. Chicago: American Library Association, 1989.

    This book presents information on planning and evaluating middle school media programs. It offers procedures in library program development as well as ways of correlating library skills with classroom instruction.

38. Smith, Jane B. *Achieving A Curriculum-Based Library Media Center Program: The Middle School Model for Change*. Chicago: American Library Association, 1995.

    This book presents information and practical models for integrating information skills into the school curriculum. This is a sequel to Smith's *Library Media Center Programs for Middle Schools.*

39. Stein, Barbara L. and Risa W. Brown. *Running A School Library Media Center: A How-to-do-it Manual for Librarians. 2nd ed.* NY: Neal-Schuman Publishers, 2002.

    A practical handbook includes chapters on getting started, administration, ordering and processing materials, cataloging, circulation, maintaining the collection, hiring and working with staff, designing and using the facility, and programming the media center.

40. Sutherland, Zena. *Children and Books.* 9th ed. Boston: Allyn & Bacon, 1997.

    Chapter One of Part One, "Children and Books Today," discusses the child psychology theories and their application to cognitive development. Chapter Two, "Guiding Children's Book Selection," discusses evaluation standards and examines the elements and range of children's literature. Subsequent chapters provide titles and summaries of recommended literature for various age groups.

41. Talab, Rosemary. *Commonsense Copyright.* NY: McFarland, 1999.

    A practical guide to applying copyright laws in school environments, one chapter specifically addressing media centers.

42. Taylor, Arlene G. *Introduction to Cataloging and Classification.* 10th ed. Libraries Unlimited, 2006.

    A basic primer on cataloging techniques and classification systems.

43. Turner, Philip. *Helping Teachers Teach: A School Library Media Specialist's Role.* 3rd ed. Englewood, CO: Libraries Unlimited, 2003.

    An exploration of the school library media specialist's role as a curriculum consultant , with specific suggestions for methods to help teachers design and evaluate classroom lessons using media resources. Also provides information on professional collection development, instructional materials selection and evaluation, and in-house workshop design. Revised in 2003.

44. Bishop, Kay. *The Collection Program in Schools: Concepts, Practices, and Information Sources.* 4th ed. Englewood, CO: Libraries Unlimited, 2007.

    A textbook for media professionals on collection development. Divided into three parts: *The Setting* covers issues, procedures, and policies; *Selection of Materials* addresses selection criteria; and *Administrative Concerns* covers acquisition, maintenance, evaluation, and meeting special needs.

45. Van Vliet, Lucille W. *Media Skills for Middle Schools: Strategies for Library Media Specialists and Teachers.* Englewood, CO: Libraries Unlimited, 1900.

    Another good source for lessons on teaching information skills. It offers subject related activities for required and elective subjects as well as discussing the aspects of instruction.

46. Wehmeyer, Lillian B. *The School Librarian as Educator.* 2nd ed. Englewood, CO: Libraries Unlimited, 1984.

    A text that examines the school library media specialist's role as instructor, offering practical suggestions for library skills instruction and including appendices with games and activities appropriate to both elementary and secondary media centers.

47. Winn, Patricia. *Integration of the Secondary School Library Media Center into the Curriculum.* Englewood, CO: Libraries Unlimited, 1991.

    This title specifically addresses the role of the media specialist in integrating the media program into the curriculum and some methods to use.

48. Woolls, E. Blanche and David V. Loertscher (Eds.). *The Microcomputer Facility and the School Library Media Specialist.* Chicago, IL: American Library Association, 1986.

    This book is a series of essays in four areas: planning the facility, operating the facility, services of the facility, and working with the facility. From district level networks to microcomputers used for circulation, the microcomputer is here presented as a tool to ease the burden of library media management.

49. Wright, Kieth. *The Challenge of Technology-Action Strategies for the School Library Media Specialist.* Chicago.: American Library Association, 1993.

    Wright wrote this book because of a concern that technology be used appropriately in education. It addresses the challenges that new technologies have created for the media professional, discusses techniques that schools or districts have used to deal with these challenges, and suggests ways that school library media specialists can prioritize their growing responsibilities.

Sample Test

DIRECTIONS: Read each item and select the best response.

1. **Who among the following is NOT an expert in child development?**
   (Skill 1.1) (Rigorous)

   A. Lawrence Kohlberg

   B. James Naisbitt

   C. Jean Piaget

   D. Erik Erikson

2. **Which version of *Information Power* was published in 1998?**
   (Skill 1.1) (Easy)

   A. *Information Power: The Role of the School Library Media Program*

   B. *Information Power: A Review of Research*

   C. *Information Power: Guidelines for School Library Media Programs*

   D. *Information Power: Building Partnerships for Learning*

3. **The TAXONOMIES OF THE SCHOOL LIBRARY MEDIA PROGRAM outlines eleven levels of school library media specialists' involvement with curriculum and instruction and was developed by:**
   (Skill 1.1) (Rigorous)

   A. Eisenberg

   B. Bloom

   C. Loertscher

   D. Lance

4. **Which of the following is an example of quantitative data that would be used to evaluate a school library media program?**
   (Skill 1.2) (Average Rigor)

   A. personnel evaluations

   B. usage statistics

   C. surveys

   D. interviews

5. An accredited elementary school has maintained an acceptable number of items in its print collection for ten years. In the evaluation review, this fact is evidence of both:
(Skill 1.2) (Rigorous)

   A. diagnostic and projective standards

   B. diagnostic and quantitative standards

   C. projective and quantitative standards

   D. projective and qualitative standards

6. The principal is completing the annual report. He needs to include substantive data on use of the media center. In addition to the number of book circulations, he would like to know the proportionate use of the media center's facilities and services by the various grade levels or content areas. This information can most quickly be obtained from:
(Skill 1.2) (Rigorous)

   A. the class scheduling log

   B. student surveys

   C. lesson plans

   D. inventory figures

7. A statement defining the core principles of a school library media program is called the:
(Skill 1.2) (Average Rigor)

   A. mission

   B. policy

   C. procedure

   D. objective

8. According to accreditation standards, school libraries should have a minimum of _____ books per student.
(Skill 1.3) (Easy)

   A. 15

   B. 12

   C. 10

   D. 5

9. In a school with one full-time library media assistant (clerk), which of the following are responsibilities of the assistant?
(Skill 1.3) (Average Rigor)

   A. selecting and ordering titles for the print collection

   B. performing circulation tasks and processing new materials

   C. in-servicing teachers on the integration of media materials into the school curriculum

   D. planning and implementing programs to involve parents and community

10. Which of the following tasks should a volunteer NOT be asked to perform?
(Skill 1.3) (Average Rigor)

   A. decorating bulletin boards

   B. demonstrating use of retrieval systems

   C. maintaining bookkeeping records

   D. fundraising

11. AASL/AECT guidelines recommend that student library aides be:
(Skill 1.3) (Average Rigor)

   A. rewarded with grades or certificates for their service

   B. allowed to assist only during free time

   C. allowed to perform para-professional duties

   D. assigned tasks that relate to maintaining the atmosphere of the media center

12. The most efficient method of evaluating support staff is to:
(Skill 1.3) (Average Rigor)

   A. administer a written test

   B. survey faculty they serve

   C. observe their performance

   D. obtain verbal confirmation during an employee interview

13. According to *Information Power*, which of the following is NOT a responsibility of the school library media specialist?
    (Skill 1.3) (Rigorous)

    A. maintaining and repairing equipment

    B. instructing educators and parents in the use of library media resources

    C. providing efficient retrieval systems for materials and equipment

    D. planning and implementing the library media center budget

14. The most appropriate means of obtaining extra funds for library media programs is:
    (Skill 1.3) (Average Rigor)

    A. having candy sales

    B. conducting book fairs

    C. charging fines

    D. soliciting donations

15. In formulating an estimated collection budget consider all of the following EXCEPT:
    (Skill 1.3) (Rigorous)

    A. attrition by loss, damage, or age

    B. the maximum cost of item replacement

    C. the number of students served

    D. the need for expansion to meet minimum guidelines

16. Which of the following is the least effective way of communicating school library media policies, procedures, and rules to media center patrons?
    (Skill 1.4) (Average Rigor)

    A. announcements made in faculty and parent support group meetings

    B. a published faculty procedures manual

    C. written guidelines in the student handbook or special media handbill

    D. a videotape orientation viewed over the school's closed circuit television system

17. Which of the following is a library policy, not a procedure?
    (Skill 1.4) (Rigorous)

    A. providing a vehicle for the circulation of audiovisual equipment

    B. setting guidelines for collection development

    C. determining the method for introducing an objective into the school improvement plan

    D. setting categorical limits on operating expenses

18. A policy is:
    (Skill 1.4) (Easy)

    A. a course of action taken to execute a plan

    B. a written statement of principle used to guarantee a management practice

    C. a statement of core values of an organization

    D. a regulation concerning certification

19. Contemporary library media design models should consider which of the following an optional need?
    (Skill 1.5) (Rigorous)

    A. flexibility of space to allow for reading, viewing, and listening

    B. space for large group activities such as district meetings, standardized testing, and lectures

    C. traffic flow patterns for entrance and exit from the media center as well as easy movement within the center

    D. adequate and easy to rearrange storage areas for the variety of media formats and packaging style of modern materials

20. According to accreditation standards, what percentage of any library's floor space should be devoted to a *professional library?*
    (Skill 1.5) (Rigorous)

    A. 3 square feet per student

    B. 2 square feet per student

    C. 1 square foot per student

    D. no minimum required

21. The most important consideration in the design of a new school library media center is:
    (Skill 1.5) (Average Rigor)

    A. the goals of the library media center program

    B. the location of the facility on the school campus

    C. state standards for facilities use

    D. the demands of current technologies

22. The process of discarding worn or outdated books and materials is known as:
    (Skill 2.1) (Easy)

    A. weeding

    B. inventory

    C. collection mapping

    D. eliminating

23. Which of the following is NOT one of three general criteria for selection of all materials?
    (Skill 2.1) (Average Rigor)

    A. authenticity

    B. appeal

    C. appropriateness

    D. allocation

24. Collection development policies are developed to accomplish all of the following EXCEPT:
    (Skill 2.1) (Rigorous)

    A. guarantee users freedom to access information

    B. recognize the needs and interests of users

    C. coordinate selection criteria and budget concerns

    D. recognize rights of individuals or groups to challenge these policies

25. Which of these Dewey Decimal classifications should be weeded most often?
    (Skill 2.1) (Rigorous)

    A. 100s

    B. 500s

    C. 700s

    D. Biographies

26. The practice of examining the quantity and quality of the school library media resource collection that provides a "snapshot" of the collection is called:
    (Skill 2.1) (Easy)

    A. collection development

    B. collection maintenance

    C. collection mapping

    D. weeding

27. Which periodical contains book reviews of currently published children and young adult books?
    (Skill 2.2) (Rigorous)

    A. *Phi Delta Kappan*

    B. *School Library Journal*

    C. *School Library Media Quarterly*

    D. *American Teacher*

28. *The Horn Book* is:
    (Skill 2.2) (Average Rigor)

    A. a book about trumpets

    B. a children's picture book

    C. a professional journal

    D. a source for resource reviews

29. In which bibliographic field should information concerning the format of an audiovisual material appear?
    (Skill 2.2) (Rigorous)

    A. material specific details

    B. physical description

    C. notes

    D. standard numbers

30. Which of these publications does not contain reviews for various types of publications:
    (Skill 2.2) (Average Rigor)

    A. *School Library Journal*

    B. *Booklist*

    C. *Media Center Review*

    D. *The Horn Book*

31. MARC is the acronym for:
    (Skill 2.2) (Easy)

    A. Mobile Accessible Recorded Content

    B. Machine Accessible Readable Content

    C. Machine Readable Content

    D. Mobile Accessible Readable Content

32. AACR2 is the acronym for:
    (Skill 2.2) (Easy)

    A. *Anglo-American Cataloging Rules Second Edition*

    B. *American Association of Cataloging Rules Second Edition*

    C. *American Association of Content Rules Second Edition*

    D. *Anglo-American Content Rules Second Edition*

33. When selecting computer information databases for library media center computers, which of the following is the least important consideration?
    (Skill 2.3) (Average Rigor)

    A. cost

    B. format

    C. user friendliness

    D. ability levels of users

34. When determining a specific piece of equipment to purchase, the school library media specialist should first consult:
    (Skill 2.3) (Average Rigor)

    A. local vendors for a demonstration

    B. reviews in technology periodicals

    C. manufacturers' catalogs for specifications

    D. the state bid list for price

35. Which of the following media should be included in the school library media center's resource collection?
    (Skill 2.3) (Rigorous)

    A. audio recordings

    B. periodicals

    C. online resources

    D. all of the above

36. Which of the following is a book jobber often used by school libraries:
   (Skill 2.4) (Rigorous)

   A. Library Media Book Services

   B. Baker and Taylor

   C. Mead and Blackwell

   D. Elementary Book Services

37. What is the best way to prepare a book order to ensure all monies are utilized?
   (Skill 2.4) (Rigorous)

   A. prepare a list of books for the exact amount of the order

   B. prepare a list that exceeds the total funds available by 10%

   C. prepare a list of books and include a list of alternate titles in case the ones on the first list aren't available

   D. select a list of books and include the following line on the order, "Do Not Exceed This Amount" (the amount of the order)

38. When a book order is received the first thing that should be done is:
   (Skill 2.4) (Average Rigor)

   A. check the order against the invoice to make sure all items have been received

   B. catalog the books

   C. place the books on the shelves

   D. notify teachers that new books have arrived

39. A catalog that contains materials from several library collections is known as a:
   (Skill 2.5) (Easy)

   A. shared catalog

   B. cooperative catalog

   C. union Catalog

   D. universal catalog

40. The most efficient method of assessing which students are users or non-users of the library media center is reviewing:
    (Skill 2.5) (Average Rigor)

    A. patron circulation records

    B. needs assessment surveys of students

    C. monthly circulation statistics

    D. the accession book for the current year.

41. OCLC is the acronym for:
    (Skill 2.5) (Average Rigor)

    A. Online Computer Library Center

    B. Online Computer Library Catalog

    C. Online Computer Library Conference

    D. Online Computer Library Content

42. In what area of a bibliographic record can the name of the author be found?
    (Skill 2.5) (Average Rigor)

    A. physical description area

    B. publication area

    C. terms of availability area

    D. title and statement of responsibility area

43. In MARC records the title information can be found under which tag?
    (Skill 2.5) (Rigorous)

    A. 130

    B. 245

    C. 425

    D. 520

44. Which of the following is not a component of a bibliographic record?
    (Skill 2.5) (Rigorous)

    A. notes

    B. call number

    C. cover image

    D. physical description area

45. According to research on promotion techniques and support for library media programs, their staunchest ally must be the:
    (Skill 2.6) (Easy)

    A. teaching faculty

    B. student body

    C. district media supervisor

    D. school principal

46. Which of the following are examples of ways to promote the school library media programs:
    (Skill 2.6) (Easy)

    A. attend school board meetings

    B. serve on the school's curriculum committee

    C. invite school board members to media planning meetings

    D. all of the above

47. All but which of the following criteria are used when determining fair use of copyrighted material for classroom use?
    (Skill 3.1) (Average Rigor)

    A. Brevity Test

    B. Spontaneity Test

    C. Time Test

    D. Cumulative Effect Test

48. All of the following are periodical directories EXCEPT:
    (Skill 3.1) (Average Rigor)

    A. *Ulrich's*

    B. *TNYT*

    C. *SIRS*

    D. *PAIS*

49. Which professional journal is published by the American Association of School Librarians?
    (Skill 3.1) (Average Rigor)

    A. *School Library Media Research*

    B. *Library Trends*

    C. *Library Power*

    D. *Voices of Youth Advocate*

50. All of the following should be housed in the reference collection EXCEPT:
    (Skill 3.1) (Easy)

    A. atlas

    B. dictionary

    C. picture book

    D. collection of encyclopedias

51. The Caldecott Medal was awarded to which book in 2002?
    (Skill 3.2) (Rigorous)

    A. *The Three Pigs* by David Wiesner

    B. *Joseph Had a Little Overcoat* by Simms Taback

    C. *Golem* by David Wisniewski

    D. *Officer Buckle and Gloria* by Peggy Rathmann

52. Which writer composes young adult literature in the fantasy genre?
    (Skill 3.2) (Rigorous)

    A. Stephen King

    B. Piers Anthony

    C. Virginia Hamilton

    D. Phyllis Whitney

53. Which fiction genre do these authors represent: Isaac Asimov, Louise Lawrence, and Andre Norton?
    (Skill 3.2) (Rigorous)

    A. adventure

    B. romance

    C. science fiction

    D. fantasy

54. This award was first presented to its namesake in 1954. This bronze medal award honors an author or illustrator whose books were published in the United States and have made a lasting contribution to literature for children. This award is known as the:
    (Skill 3.2) (Rigorous)

    A. Newbery Medal

    B. Laura Ingalls Wilder Award

    C. Mildred L. Batchelder Award

    D. Carnegie Medal

55. All of the following are authors of young adult fiction EXCEPT:
    (Skill 3.2) (Rigorous)

    A. Paul Zindel

    B. Norma Fox Mazer

    C. S.E. Hinton

    D. Maurice Sendak

56. All of the following are authors of fantasy EXCEPT:
    (Skill 3.2) (Rigorous)

    A. Ray Bradbury

    B. Ursula K. Le Guin

    C. Piers Anthony

    D. Ann McCaffrey

57. The award given for the best children's literature (text) is the:
    (Skill 3.2) (Easy)

    A. Caldecott Medal

    B. Newbery Medal

    C. Pulitzer

    D. Booklist

58. In recognition of outstanding translations of children's books this award was created in 1966. It is presented to the publisher that is responsible for translating the work into English.
    (Skill 3.2) (Average Rigor)

    A. Newbery Medal

    B. Laura Ingalls Wilder Award

    C. Mildred L. Batchelder Award

    D. Carnegie Medal

59. Which of the following file extensions does not represent an image file?
    (Skill 3.3) (Average Rigor)

    A. .jpeg

    B. .gif

    C. .csv

    D. .bmp

60. Which of the following has made the greatest impact on school library media centers in the last decade? *(Skill 3.3) (Average Rigor)*

    A. censorship

    B. emerging technologies

    C. learning style research

    D. state funding reductions

61. USB is the acronym for: *(Skill 3.3) (Average Rigor)*

    A. United Streaming Business

    B. Universal Serial Bus

    C. United Serial Business

    D. Universal Streaming Bus

62. A periodical index search that allows the user to pair Keywords with <u>and</u>, <u>but</u>, or <u>or</u> is called: *(Skill 3.4) (Rigorous)*

    A. Boolean

    B. dialoguing

    C. wildcarding

    D. truncation

63. A request from a social studies teacher for the creation of a list of historical fiction titles for a book report assignment is a _____ request. *(Skill 3.4) (Average Rigor)*

    A. ready reference

    B. research

    C. specific needs

    D. complex search

64. Resources can be shared within a small geographic location such as a school by the use of a: *(Skill 3.5) (Average Rigor)*

    A. SWN

    B. MAN

    C. LAN

    D. WAN

65. All of the following are benefits of interlibrary loan EXCEPT:
(Skill 3.5) (Rigorous)

A. maximizing the use media center funds

B. providing a wider range of resources available for patrons

C. building partnerships with outside agencies

D. eliminating the need for media assistants

66. A network allows which of the following to occur?
(Skill 3.5) (Average Rigor)

A. sharing files

B. sharing printers

C. sharing software

D. all of the above

67. A group of students in the business club will be creating a website to sell their product. When selecting their domain name, which of the following extensions would be best to use?
(Skill 3.6) (Rigorous)

A. .com

B. .edu

C. .cfm

D. .html

68. An online database that provides print and electronic journal subscriptions is:
(Skill 3.6) (Rigorous)

A. Kids Connect

B. KQWeb

C. EBSCO

D. NICEM

69. Instruction provided via satellite or cable television is called:
    (Skill 3.7) (Average Rigor)

    A. home study

    B. distance learning

    C. extension services

    D. telecommunications

70. Advantages of distance education include all of the following EXCEPT:
    (Skill 3.7) (Rigorous)

    A. students can access and respond to information outside of a normal schedule

    B. students have fewer choices regarding content

    C. homebound students may receive instruction

    D. it may be more cost effective to use distance learning than to hire a teacher

71. The media specialist needs to expand the collection to include a wider variety of resources for visually impaired students. Which of the following would be least beneficial?
    (Skill 3.8) (Average Rigor)

    A. books with larger print

    B. books in Braille format

    C. books in audio format

    D. Books in video format

72. *Information Power: Building Partnerships for Learning* recommends flexible scheduling for:
    (Skill 3.9) (Easy)

    A. elementary school library media centers

    B. middle school library media centers

    C. secondary school library media centers

    D. all school library media centers

73. When creating a schedule for a school library media center the type of schedule that maximizes access to resources is:
    (Skill 3.9) (Easy)

    A. fixed schedule

    B. open schedule

    C. partial fixed schedule

    D. flexible schedule

74. The school library media center should be an inviting space that encourages learning. To accomplish this the school library media specialist should do all of the following EXCEPT:
    (Skill 3.10) (Average Rigor)

    A. collaborate with school staff and students

    B. create a schedule where each class comes to the media center each week for instruction

    C. arrange materials so that they are easy to locate

    D. promote the program as a wonderful place for learning

75. A secondary school social studies teacher reads an article in the current month's *Smithsonian* that clarifies points in the unit of study on the day prior to the scheduled unit test. He asks the media specialist if copyright law would allow copying the entire 3100 word article for distribution to each student in his two honors American history classes. The media specialist's proper response is:
    (Skill 3.11) (Rigorous)

    A. he can make only one copy and read it to the class

    B. he may not copy it because of the word length

    C. he may excerpt sections of it to meet the brevity test

    D. he may copy the needed multiples, allowed by the spontaneity test

76. Section 108 of the Copyright Act permits the copying of an entire book if three conditions are met. Which of the following is NOT one of those conditions?
    (Skill 3.11) (Rigorous)

    A. The library intends to allow inter-library loan of the book.

    B. The library is an archival library.

    C. The copyright notice appears on all the copies.

    D. The library is a public library.

77. Under the copyright brevity test, an educator may reproduce without written permission:
    (Skill 3.11) (Rigorous)

    A. 10% of any prose or poetry work

    B. 500 words from a 5000 word article

    C. 240 words of a 2400 word story

    D. no work over 2500 words

78. Licensing has become a popular means of copyright protection in the area of:
    (Skill 3.11) (Average Rigor)

    A. duplicating books for interlibrary loan

    B. use of software application on multiple machines

    C. music copying

    D. making transparency copies of books or workbooks that are too expensive to purchase.

79. "Fair Use" policy in videotaping off-air from commercial television requires:
    (Skill 3.11) (Rigorous)

    A. material should be shown within 5 days, and erased by the 20th day

    B. material should be shown within 10 days and erased by the 30th day

    C. material should be shown within 10 days and erased by the 45th day

    D. there are no restrictions

80. The English I (9th Grade) teacher wants his students to become familiar with the contents of books in the reference area of the school library media center. He asks the library media specialist to recommend an activity to accomplish this goal. Which of the following activities would best achieve the goal?
    (Skill 4.1) (Average Rigor)

    A. assign a research paper on a specific social issues topic

    B. require a biography of a famous person

    C. design a set of questions covering a variety of topics and initiate a scavenger hunt approach to their location

    D. teach students the Dewey Decimal system and have them list several books in each Dewey subcategory

81. Several Skills in *Information Skills* ... are worded exactly the same from K-12 because the students' mastery of the skill depends on performing that skill at ever advancing levels, even beyond graduation. Which of the following is one of those same worded skills?
    (Skill 4.1) (Rigorous)

    A. examine award-winning materials

    B. identify parts of a book

    C. use materials without violating copyright laws

    D. use appropriate sources to locate information

82. According to AASL/AECT guidelines, in her role as *instructional consultant*, the school library media specialist uses her expertise to:
    (Skill 4.1) (Average Rigor)

    A. assist teachers in acquiring information skills that they can incorporate into classroom instruction

    B. provide access to resource sharing systems

    C. plan lessons in media production

    D. provide staff development activities in equipment use

83. An elementary teacher, planning a unit on the local environment, finds materials that are too global or above her students' ability level. The best solution to this problem is to:
(Skill 4.1) (Rigorous)

   A. broaden the scope of the study to emphasize global concerns

   B. eliminate the unit from the content

   C. replace the unit with another unit that teaches the same skills

   D. have the students design their own study materials using media production techniques

84. In assessing learning styles for staff development, consider that adults:
(Skill 4.1) (Rigorous)

   A. are less affected by the learning environment than children

   B. are more receptive to performing in and in front of groups

   C. learn better when external motivations are guaranteed.

   D. demand little feedback

85. A high school science teacher is about to begin a frog dissection unit. Three students refuse to participate. When asked for assistance, the library media specialist should:
(Skill 4.1) (Rigorous)

   A. work with the teacher to design a replacement unit with print and non-print material on frog anatomy

   B. offer to allow the student to use the library as a study hall during their class time

   C. recommend that the student be sent to another class studying frogs without dissecting

   D. abstain from condoning the student's refusal to work

86. The most effective method of initiating closer contacts with and determining the needs of classroom teachers is to:
    (Skill 4.2) (Average Rigor)

    A. ask to be included on the agenda of periodic faculty meetings

    B. present after school or weekend in-services in opening communication channels

    C. request permission to be included in grade-level or content-area meetings

    D. establish a library advisory committee with one representative from each grade level or content area

87. To foster the collaborative process the media specialist must possess all of the following skills EXCEPT:
    (Skill 4.2) (Easy)

    A. leadership

    B. flexibility

    C. perversity

    D. persistence

88. In most learning hierarchies, which of the following is the highest order critical thinking skill?
    (Skill 4.3) (Average Rigor)

    A. appreciation

    B. inference

    C. recall

    D. comprehension

89. After reading *The Pearl,* a tenth grader asks, "Why can't we start sentences with *and* like John Steinbeck?" This student is showing the ability to:
    (Skill 4.3) (Rigorous)

    A. appreciate

    B. comprehend

    C. infer

    D. evaluate

90. Howard Gardner created:
    (Skill 4.3) (Easy)

    A. Multiple Intelligences

    B. Taxonomies of Learning

    C. Big6 Model

    D. @ Your Library

91. A kindergarten class has just viewed a video on alligators. The best way to evaluate the suitability of the material for this age group is to:
    (Skill 4.4) (Rigorous)

    A. test the students' ability to recall the main points of the video

    B. compare this product to other similar products on this content

    C. observe the body language and verbal comments during the viewing

    D. ask the children to comment on the quality of the video at the end of the viewing

92. Students' reading habits can be evaluated by use of which of the following:
    (Skill 4.4) (Easy)

    A. student surveys

    B. interviews

    C. standardized tests

    D. all of the above

93. Which of the following would be the best way to acclimate a media center volunteer to the workings of the media center is to:
    (Skill 4.5) (Average Rigor)

    A. provide the volunteer with a brochure regarding the workings of the media center

    B. provide the volunteer with a manual that outlines their duties

    C. provide a hands-on orientation session for the volunteer

    D. provide a video for the volunteer that outlines their duties

94. As much as possible, information skills should be taught as:
    (Skill 4.6) (Easy)

    A. lessons independent of content studies

    B. lessons to supplement content studies

    C. lessons integrated into content studies.

    D. lessons enriched by content studies

95. The creators of the Big6 Model are:
    (Skill 4.6) (Average Rigor)

    A. Eisenberg and Berkowitz

    B. Marzano and Bloom

    C. Bloom and Gardner

    D. Lance and Eisenberg

96. When evaluating resources for effectiveness it is important to consider all of the following EXCEPT:
    (Skill 4.7) (Average Rigor)

    A. style of the web page

    B. the intended audience

    C. whether or not the site is from a scholarly source

    D. the scope of the information

97. Which of the following searches would most likely return the most results?
    (Skill 4.7) (Average Rigor)

    A. lions and tigers

    B. lions not tigers

    C. lions or tigers

    D. lions and not tigers

98. The first step in planning a training program for untrained support staff is:
    (Skill 5.1) (Rigorous)

    A. assessing the employee's existing skills

    B. identifying and prioritizing skills from the job description/ evaluation instrument

    C. determining the time schedule for the completion of training

    D. studying the resume and speak to former employers

99. Staff development activities in the use of materials and equipment are most effective if they:
    (Skill 5.1) (Average Rigor)

    A. are conducted individually as need is expressed

    B. are sequenced in difficulty of operation or use

    C. result in use of the acquired skills in classroom lessons

    D. are evaluated for effectiveness

100. Staff development is most effective when it includes:
(Skill 5.1) (Average Rigor)

A. continuing support

B. hand-outs

C. video tutorials

D. stated objectives

101. Which of the following is the most desirable learning outcome of a staff development workshop on *Teaching with Interactive DVDS*? Participants:
(Skill 5.1) (Average Rigor)

A. score 80% or better on a post-test

B. design content specific lessons from multiple resources

C. sign up to take additional workshops

D. encourage other teachers to participate in future workshops

102. Which of the following resources delineates eleven levels of involvement of the school library media center?
(Skill 5.2) (Rigorous)

A. *Administering the School Library Media Center*

B. *Information Power*

C. *Taxonomies of the School Library Media Center*

D. *School Library Media Annual*

103. All of the following organizations serve school libraries EXCEPT:
(Skill 5.2) (Average Rigor)

A. AASL

B. AECT

C. ALCT

D. ALA

TEACHER CERTIFICATION STUDY GUIDE

104. National guidelines for school library media programs are generally developed by all of the following EXCEPT:
 (Skill 5.2) (Easy)

    A. AASL

    B. ALA

    C. AECT

    D. NECT

105. Which publication offers research-based scholarly articles?
 (Skill 5.2) (Rigorous)

    A. *School Library Media Quarterly*

    B. *Media and Methods*

    C. *TechTrends*

    D. *Megatrends*

106. IRA is the acronym for the:
 (Skill 5.3) (Easy)

    A. Interactive Reading Administration

    B. International Reading Administration

    C. International Reading Association

    D. Interactive Reading Association

107. All of the following are areas in which the school library media specialist supports the learning community EXCEPT:
 (Skill 5.4) (Average Rigor)

    A. technician

    B. collaboration

    C. leadership

    D. technology

108. Current judicial rulings on censorship issues will most likely be discussed in:
 (Skill 5.5) (Average Rigor)

    A. *Kirkus Reviews*

    B. *School Library Media Review*

    C. *New Media*

    D. *Newsletter of Intellectual Freedom*

109. Which associations created the Library Bill of Rights and the Code of Ethics?
 (Skill 5.5) (Rigorous)

    A. AASL and AECT

    B. ALA and AECT

    C. ALA and AASL

    D. ALA and NCTE

110. A student looks for a specific title on domestic violence. When he learns it is overdue, he asks the library media specialist to tell him the borrower's name. The library media specialist should first:
(Skill 5.5) (Rigorous)

   A. readily reveal the borrower's name

   B. suggest he look for the book in another library

   C. offer to put the boy's name on reserve pending the book's return

   D. offer to request an interlibrary loan

111. Freedom of access of information for children includes all of the following EXCEPT:
(Skill 5.5) (Average Rigor)

   A. development of critical thinking

   B. reflection of social growth

   C. provision for religious differences

   D. discrimination of different points of view

112. The Library Bill of Rights includes all of the following EXCEPT:
(Skill 5.5) (Average Rigor)

   A. information presented in a library should be selected based upon the age level of the students

   B. resources should include a representation of all ideas, concepts, and backgrounds

   C. resources should not be excluded because of viewpoint

   D. censorship should be challenged

113. AECT's Code of Ethics contains which of the following sections?
(Skill 5.5) (Average Rigor)

   A. Commitment to Media

   B. Commitment to Education

   C. Commitment to Society

   D. Commitment to School

114. **The Right to Read Statement was issued by:**
    (Skill 5.5) (Rigorous)

    A. AECT

    B. ALA

    C. NCTE

    D. NICEM

115. **Instructional materials are evolving into all of the following formats EXCEPT:**
    (Skill 5.6) (Easy)

    A. ebooks

    B. online magazines

    C. audio cassettes

    D. interactive software

116. **Current trends in school library media include all of the following EXCEPT:**
    (Skill 5.6) (Easy)

    A. collaboration

    B. face-to-face instruction

    C. flexible scheduling

    D. technology integration

117. **Which of the following is part of the American Library Association's Advocacy Toolkit?**
    (Skill 5.7) (Easy)

    A. @ Your Library

    B. Code of Ethics

    C. Information Power

    D. Taxonomies of Learning

118. **This outlines the role of the school library media specialist and the programs they manage.**
    (Skill 5.7) (Average Rigor)

    A. Taxonomies of Learning

    B. Code of Ethics

    C. @ Your Library

    D. Library Bill of Rights

119. **Must have been teaching for three years, hold a bachelor's degree and have a valid teaching license are eligibility requirements for:**
    (Skill 5.8) (Easy)

    A. Library Media Specialist

    B. Curriculum Specialist

    C. National Board Certification

    D. none of the above

120. A school with 500–749 students should have how many media specialists?
 (Skill 5.8) (Easy)

 A. 1 part-time media specialist

 B. 1 full time media specialist

 C. 2 full time media specialist

 D. no media specialist required

121. Which of the following is the best description of the ALA recommendations for certification for a school library media specialist?
 (Skill 5.8) (Rigorous)

 A. a bachelor's degree in any content area plus 30 hours of library/information science

 B. a master's degree from an accredited Educational Media program

 C. a bachelor's degree in library/information science and a master's degree in any field of education

 D. a master's degree from an accredited Library and Information Studies program

122. The federal law enacted by Congress in December 2000 that imposed specific Internet restrictions on schools that receive Federal E-rate funding is known as:
 (Skill 5.9) (Average Rigor)

 A. CIP

 B. CIPA

 C. SIP

 D. AUP

123. When a parent complains about the content of a specific title in a library media collection, the library media specialist's first course of action in responding to the complaint is to:
 (Skill 5.9) (Rigorous)

 A. remove the title from the shelf and purge it from both the catalog and the shelf list

 B. place the book in reserve status for circulation at parent request only

 C. submit the complaint to a district review committee

 D. explain the principles of intellectual freedom to the complaining parent

124. Funded under the No Child Left Behind Act, this program helps LEAs improve reading achievement by providing increased access to up-to-date school library materials including technologically advanced school library media centers and professionally certified school library media specialists.
(Skill 5.9) (Rigorous)

A. 21st Century Schools

B. Improving Literacy Through School Libraries

C. @ Your Library

D. Technology in the 21st Century

125. In the landmark U.S. Supreme Court ruling in favor of Pico, the court's opinion established that:
(Skill 5.9) (Rigorous)

A. library books, being optional not required reading, could not be arbitrarily removed by school boards

B. school boards have the same jurisdiction over library books as they have over textbooks

C. the intent to remove pervasively vulgar material is the same as the intent to deny free access to ideas

D. First Amendment challenges in regards to library books are the responsibility of appeals courts

TEACHER CERTIFICATION STUDY GUIDE

Answer Key

1.	B	33.	A	65.	D	97.	C
2.	D	34.	C	66.	D	98.	B
3.	C	35.	D	67.	A	99.	C
4.	B	36.	B	68.	C	100.	A
5.	B	37.	D	69.	B	101.	B
6.	A	38.	A	70.	B	102.	C
7.	A	39.	C	71.	D	103.	C
8.	C	40.	A	72.	D	104.	D
9.	B	41.	A	73.	C	105.	A
10.	C	42.	C	74.	B	106.	C
11.	A	43.	B	75.	D	107.	A
12.	C	44.	C	76.	A	108.	D
13.	A	45.	D	77.	B	109.	B
14.	B	46.	D	78.	B	110.	C
15.	B	47.	C	79.	C	111.	C
16.	A	48.	B	80.	C	112.	A
17.	B	49.	A	81.	D	113.	C
18.	B	50.	C	82.	D	114.	C
19.	B	51.	A	83.	D	115.	C
20.	C	52.	B	84.	B	116.	B
21.	A	53.	C	85.	A	117.	A
22.	A	54.	B	86.	C	118.	C
23.	D	55.	D	87.	C	119.	C
24.	C	56.	A	88.	A	120.	B
25.	B	57.	B	89.	D	121.	D
26.	C	58.	C	90.	A	122.	B
27.	B	59.	C	91.	C	123.	D
28.	D	60.	B	92.	D	124.	B
29.	C	61.	B	93.	C	125.	A
30.	C	62.	A	94.	C		
31.	C	63.	C	95.	A		
32.	A	64.	C	96.	A		

LIBRARY MEDIA

Rigor Table

	Easy 20%	Average Rigor 40%	Rigorous 40%
Question #	2, 8, 18, 22, 26, 31, 32, 39, 45, 46, 50, 57, 72, 73, 87, 90, 92, 94, 104, 106, 115, 116, 117, 119, 120	4, 7, 9, 10, 11, 12, 14, 16, 21, 23, 28, 30, 33, 34, 38, 40, 41, 42, 47, 48, 49, 59, 60, 61, 63, 64, 66, 69, 71, 74, 78, 80, 82, 86, 88, 93, 95, 96, 97, 99, 100, 101, 103, 107, 108, 111, 112, 113, 118, 122	1, 3, 5, 6, 13, 15, 17, 19, 20, 24, 25, 27, 29, 35, 36, 37, 43, 44, 51, 52, 53, 54, 55, 56, 58, 62, 65, 67, 68, 70, 75, 76, 77, 79, 81, 83, 84, 85, 89, 91, 98, 102, 105, 109, 110, 114, 121, 123, 124, 125

TEACHER CERTIFICATION STUDY GUIDE

Rationales with Sample Questions

1. **Which of the following is NOT an expert in child development?**
   (Skill 1.1) (Rigorous)

   a. Lawrence Kohlberg
   b. James Naisbitt
   c. Jean Piaget
   d. Erik Erikson

   Answer: b. James Naisbitt

   Kohlberg is the developer of Modes of Learning. Piaget is one of the most influential developmental psychologists. Erik Erikson is also a well-known developmental psychologists. James Naisbitt is an author in the field of future studies making him the only one not involved in child development and Option B the best answer.

2. **Which version of *Information Power* was published in 1998?**
   (Skill 1.1) (Easy)

   a. *Information Power: The Role of the School Library Media Program*
   b. *Information Power: A Review of Research*
   c. *Information Power: Guidelines for School Library Media Programs*
   d. *Information Power: Building Partnerships for Learning*

   Answer: d. *Information Power: Building Partnerships for Learning*

   Option D is the version that was published in 1998. *Information Power: Guidelines for School Library Media Programs* was published in 1988.

3. **The TAXONOMIES OF THE SCHOOL LIBRARY MEDIA PROGRAM outlines eleven levels of school library media specialists' involvement with curriculum and instruction and was developed by:**
   (Skill 1.1) (Rigorous)

   a. Eisenberg
   b. Bloom
   c. Loertscher
   d. Lance

   Answer: c. Loertscher

   Eisenberg is one of the creators of the Big6 Model. Bloom was the developer of Bloom's Taxonomy. Keith Curry-Lance has conducted many studies on the effect of school library media programs on student achievement.

LIBRARY MEDIA

4. **Which of the following is an example of quantitative data that would be used to evaluate a school library media program?**
   (Skill 1.2) (Average Rigor)

   a. personnel evaluations
   b. usage statistics
   c. surveys
   d. interviews

Answer b. Usage statistics

Option B is the most appropriate answer because it is the only one listed that provides measurable data. All of the others are qualitative forms of data.

5. **An accredited elementary school has maintained an acceptable number of items in its print collection for ten years. In the evaluation review, this fact is evidence of both:**
   (Skill 1.2) (Rigorous)

   a. diagnostic and projective standards
   b. diagnostic and quantitative standards
   c. projective and quantitative standards
   d. projective and qualitative standards

Answer: b. diagnostic and quantitative standards.

Diagnostic evaluations are standards based on conditions existing in programs that have already been judged excellent. The acceptable print collection can be compared to national guidelines for diagnostic information. Quantitative evaluations involve numerical data of some kind. By taking a look at the numbers in the collection the media specialist can review collection totals. Option B is the correct answer.

6. The principal is completing the annual report. He needs to include substantive data on use of the media center. In addition to the number of book circulations, he would like to know the proportionate use of the media center's facilities and services by the various grade levels or content areas. This information can most quickly be obtained from:
(Skill 1.2) (Rigorous)

a. the class scheduling log
b. student surveys
c. lesson plans
d. inventory figures

Answer: a. the class scheduling log

One of the best tools to use to determine how the media center's facilities are being used is the schedule. Often the schedule is broken down by the various areas in the media center. Teachers may schedule the specific area(s) they need. This makes Option A the most appropriate answer.

7. A statement defining the core principles of a school library media program is called the:
(Skill 1.2) (Average Rigor)

a. mission
b. policy
c. procedure
d. objective

Answer: a. mission

The core principles of an organization are outlined in a mission statement. An objective is a specific statement of measurable result that reflects the mission statement.

8. **According Southern Association Accreditation Standards, school libraries should have a minimum of _____ books per student.**
   (Skill 1.3) (Easy)

   a. 15
   b. 12
   c. 10
   d. 5

Answer: c. 10

Southern Association Accreditation Standards state that school libraries should carry a minimum of 10 volumes per student. New schools have up to three years to meet the minimum requirements.

9. **In a school with one full-time library media assistant (clerk), which of the following are responsibilities of the assistant?**
   (Skill 1.3) (Average Rigor)

   a. selecting and ordering titles for the print collection
   b. performing circulation tasks and processing new materials
   c. in-servicing teachers on the integration of media materials into the school curriculum
   d. planning and implementing programs to involve parents and community

Answer: b. performing circulation tasks and processing new materials.

Option B is the most appropriate answer. Circulation tasks and the processing of materials generally involve clerical duties. The other options are usually performed by a licensed media specialists.

TEACHER CERTIFICATION STUDY GUIDE

10. Which of the following tasks should a volunteer NOT be asked to perform?
    (Skill 1.3) (Average Rigor)

    a. decorating bulletin boards
    b. demonstrating use of retrieval systems
    c. maintaining bookkeeping records
    d. fundraising

Answer: c. maintaining bookkeeping records.

Volunteers are crucial to the effective running of a school library media center. Their assistance is invaluable in the areas of clerical tasks, creative tasks, or promoting the media center. However, the media specialist should be responsible for maintaining bookkeeping records to ensure the budgets are managed well, making Option C the most appropriate answer.

11. *AASL/AECT guidelines recommend that student library aides be:*
    (Skill 1.3) (Average Rigor)

    a. rewarded with grades or certificates for their service
    b. allowed to assist only during free time
    c. allowed to perform paraprofessional duties
    d. assigned tasks that relate to maintaining the atmosphere of the media center

Answer: a. rewarded with grades or certificates for their service

It is important to recognize students for the valuable service they perform as student library aides. In younger grades that recognition can come in the form or certificates. High school or middle school students may be a library aide as part of their course requirements. In this case, outstanding performance would be recognized in the form of grades. Option A is the most appropriate answer.

12. **The most efficient method of evaluating support staff is to:**
    (Skill 1.3) (Average Rigor)

    a. administer a written test
    b. survey faculty whom they serve
    c. observe their performance
    d. obtain verbal confirmation during an employee interview

Answer: c. observe their performance

The most efficient method of evaluating support staff is to observe their performance. An observation can provide an overall picture of the tasks they routinely perform. Observations may be conducted by the media specialist alone or in conjunction with another school administrator or fellow media specialist.

13. **According to *Information Power*, which of the following is NOT a responsibility of the school library media specialist?**
    (Skill 1.3) (Rigorous)

    a. maintaining and repairing equipment
    b. instructing educators and parents in the use of library media resources
    c. providing efficient retrieval systems for materials and equipment
    d. planning and implementing the library media center budget

Answer: a. maintaining and repairing equipment

While the school library media specialist is responsible for program administration and aiding with instruction, their responsibilities do not include maintaining and repairing equipment. This is generally the duty of an assistant or technician

14. **The most appropriate means of obtaining extra funds for library media programs is:**
    (Skill 1.3) (Average Rigor)

    a. having candy sales
    b. conducting book fairs
    c. charging fines
    d. soliciting donations

Answer: b. conducting book fairs

The most appropriate answer for this question is Option B, conducting book fairs. This keeps in line with the main focus of a school library media program, literacy.

15. In formulating an estimated collection budget consider all of the following EXCEPT:
    (Skill 1.3) (Rigorous)

    a. attrition by loss, damage, or age
    b. the maximum cost of item replacement
    c. the number of students served
    d. the need for expansion to meet minimum guidelines

Answer: b. the maximum cost of item replacement

The first consideration for formulating a collection budget is to determine whether or not the collection meets minimum guidelines. Then decide upon the funding needed to meet the guidelines. It is also important to allot funds to replace lost or worn items. Option B, the maximum cost of item replacement is not used in formulating a collection budget making it the most appropriate answer.

16. Which of the following is the least effective way of communicating school library media policies, procedures, and rules to media center patrons?
    (Skill 1.4) (Average Rigor)

    a. announcements made in faculty and parent support group meetings
    b. a published faculty procedures manual
    c. written guidelines in the student handbook or special media handbill
    d. a videotaped orientation viewed over the school's closed circuit television system

Answer: a. announcements made in faculty and parent support group meetings

When providing information regarding policies, procedures and rules for media center patrons it is important to provide them with tangible and detailed information. With Option A, announcements at meetings, the information is not necessarily written down and the media specialist may have to rely on those present to share information with others. It is the least reliable.

TEACHER CERTIFICATION STUDY GUIDE

17. **Which of the following is a library policy, not a procedure?**
    (Skill 1.4) (Rigorous)

a. providing a vehicle for the circulation of audiovisual equipment
b. setting guidelines for collection development
c. determining the method for introducing an objective into the school improvement plan
d. setting categorical limits on operating expenses

Answer: b. setting guidelines for collection development

A policy is a plan or a course of action such as setting the guidelines for collection development as listed in Option B. A procedure is a set of specific steps or methods used to perform a specific action.

18. **A policy is:**
    (Skill 1.4) (Easy)

a. a course of action taken to execute a plan
b. a written statement of principle used to guarantee a management practice
c. a statement of core values of an organization
d. a regulation concerning certification

Answer: b. a course of action taken to execute a plan

The most appropriate answer was Option A. A procedure is a course of action taken to execute a plan. A mission is a statement of core values.

19. **Contemporary library media design models should consider which of the following an optional need?**
    (Skill 1.5) (Rigorous)

a. flexibility of space to allow for reading, viewing, and listening
b. space for large group activities such as district meetings, standardized testing, and lectures
c. traffic flow patterns for entrance and exit from the media center as well as easy movement within the center
d. adequate and easy to rearrange storage areas for the variety of media formats and packaging style of modern materials

Answer: b. space for large group activities such as district meetings, standardized testing, and lectures

Flexibility of space, traffic flow patterns that allow ease of movement, and adequate storage are all crucial to design of a media center. Therefore, Option B is the best answer. While a space for large group activities is desirable for community use, it is not vital to the operation of a school library media center.

TEACHER CERTIFICATION STUDY GUIDE

20. According to SAC standards, what percentage of any library's floor space should be devoted to a *professional library*?
    (Skill 1.5) (Rigorous)

    a. 3 square feet per student
    b. 2 square feet per student
    c. 1 square foot per student
    d. no minimum required

Answer: c. 1 square foot per student

Professional collections should occupy an area of at least 1 square foot per student. This makes Option C the most appropriate answer.

21. The most important consideration in the design of a new school library media center is:
    (Skill 1.5) (Average Rigor)

    a. the goals of the library media center program
    b. the location of the facility on the school campus
    c. state standards for facilities use
    d. the demands of current technologies

Answer: a. the goals of the library media center program

The goals of a library media program should be a most important consideration when planning a new school media center. The other options should be considered, but Option A is the most appropriate answer.

22. The process of discarding worn or outdated books and materials is known as:
    (Skill 2.1) (Easy)

    a. weeding
    b. inventory
    c. collection mapping
    d. eliminating

Answer: a. weeding

Option A is the most appropriate answer. Outdated or worn books and materials need to be removed from the library collection. This process is known as weeding.

LIBRARY MEDIA

23. Which of the following is NOT one of three general criteria for selection of all materials?
    (Skill 2.1) (Average Rigor)

a. authenticity
b. appeal
c. appropriateness
d. allocation

Answer: d. allocation

When selecting materials the school library generally looks for materials that have reliable information, appeal to students and are appropriate for the grade levels their program serves. Option D, allocation, is not one of the criteria use to select materials

24. Collection development policies are developed to accomplish all of the following EXCEPT:
    (Skill 2.1) (Rigorous)

a. guarantee users freedom to access information
b. recognize the needs and interests of users
c. coordinate selection criteria and budget concerns
d. recognize rights of individuals or groups to challenge these policies

Answer: c. coordinate selection criteria and budget concerns

The main goal of a collection development policy is to set guidelines and procedures that govern how resources are purchased and managed. It does not coordinate any criteria or address funding issues.

25. Which of these Dewey Decimal classifications should be weeded most often?
    (Skill 2.1) (Rigorous)

a. 100s
b. 500s
c. 700s
d. Biographies

Answer: b. 500s

Materials in this section need to be continuously checked to ensure that the scientific information is correct. The 100s should be weeded every five to eight years. The 700s should be kept until worn and biographies keep the most current versions.

26. The practice of examining the quantity and quality of the school library media resource collection that provides a "snapshot" of the collection is called:
(Skill 2.1) (Easy)

a. collection development
b. collection maintenance
c. collection mapping
d. weeding

Answer: c. collection mapping

Collection maps are of great benefit to the school library media specialist. They help to identify strengths and weaknesses in the collection, plan for purchases and identify areas in need of weeding. Option C is the most appropriate answer.

27. Which periodical contains book reviews of currently published children and young adult books?
(Skill 2.2) (Rigorous)

a. *Phi Delta Kappan*
b. *School Library Journal*
c. *School Library Media Quarterly*
d. *American Teacher*

Answer: b. *School Library Journal*

The *School Library Journal* is the world's largest book review source making Option B the best answer. *Phi Delta Kappan* is a professional journal for education. *School Library Media Quarterly* is a journal published by the American Library Association to assist with program administration of school library media programs. *American Teacher* is a magazine for the teaching profession.

28. *The Horn Book* is:
    (Skill 2.2) (Average Rigor)

a. a book about trumpets
b. a children's picture book
c. a professional journal
d. a source for resource reviews

Answer: d. a source for resource review

The Horn Book is a collective review resource that lists book reviews as well as listing additional places where the item has been reviewed. While it is a professional resource, it is not a professional journal. This makes Option D the most appropriate answer.

29. In which bibliographic field should information concerning the format of an audiovisual material appear?
    (Skill 2.2) (Rigorous)

a. material specific details
b. physical description
c. notes
d. standard numbers

Answer: c. Notes

Using the 500 – General Note field in a MARC record the format of the audiovisual materials can be listed. This makes Option C the most appropriate answer. The physical description contains information about the price and number of pages.

30. Which of these publications does not contain reviews for various types of publications:
    (Skill 2.2) (Average Rigor)

a. *School Library Journal*
b. *Booklist*
c. *Media Center Review*
d. *The Horn Book*

Answer: c. *Media Center Review*

The best answer is c, *Media Center Review*. All of the other publications provide reviews for books and other resources.

TEACHER CERTIFICATION STUDY GUIDE

31. **MARC is the acronym for:**
    (Skill 2.2) (Easy)

    a. Mobile Accessible Recorded Content
    b. Machine Accessible Readable Content
    c. Machine Readable Content
    d. Mobile Accessible Readable Content

Answer: c. Machine Readable Content

Option C is the most appropriate answer. MARC is the acronym for Machine Readable Content. The MARC format is used in the cataloging of resources.

32. **AACR2 is the acronym for:**
    (Skill 2.2) (Easy)

    a. Anglo-American Cataloging Rules Second Edition
    b. American Association of Cataloging Rules Second Edition
    c. American Association of Content Rules Second Edition
    d. Anglo-American Content Rules Second Edition

Answer: a. *Anglo-American Cataloging Rules Second Edition*

Option A is the most appropriate answer. AACR2 outlines specific rules that must be followed when cataloging items.

33. **When selecting computer information databases for library media center computers, which of the following is the least important consideration?**
    (Skill 2.3) (Average Rigor)

    a. cost
    b. format
    c. user friendliness
    d. ability levels of users

Answer: a. cost

When purchasing computer software it is most important to consider the end users. The software must be easy to use and meet the desired needs. Cost must be taken into consideration but it should not be the absolute determiner for purchasing software. Option A is the least important consideration.

LIBRARY MEDIA

34. **When determining a specific piece of equipment to purchase, the school library media specialist should first consult:**
    (Skill 2.3) (Average Rigor)

    a. local vendors for a demonstration
    b. reviews in technology periodicals
    c. manufacturers' catalogs for specifications
    d. the state bid list for price

    Answer: c. manufacturer's catalogs for specifications

    Before purchasing a piece of equipment, it is important to determine whether a particular piece will perform the needed task. One of the best places to find this answer is Option C, manufacturer's catalogs. The other resources may be helpful, once the basic specifications have been checked.

35. **Which of the following media should be included in the school library media center's resource collection?**
    (Skill 2.3) (Rigorous)

    a. audio recordings
    b. periodicals
    c. online resources
    d. all of the above

    Answer: d. all of the above

    A school library media collection should contain a wide array of materials in various formats. Audio recordings, periodicals, and online resources should be a par of the collection as well as many other types of resources. This makes Option D the most appropriate answer.

36. **Which of the following is a book jobber often used by school libraries:**
    (Skill 2.4) (Rigorous)

    a. Library Media Book Services
    b. Baker and Taylor
    c. Mead and Blackwell
    d. Elementary Book Services

    Answer: b. Baker and Taylor

    A jobber buys products from a manufacturer and sells it to retailers. One of the more popular book jobbers is Baker and Taylor.

TEACHER CERTIFICATION STUDY GUIDE

37. **What is the best way to prepare a book order to ensure all monies are utilized?**
    (Skill 2.4) (Rigorous)

    a. Prepare a list of books for the exact amount of the order
    b. Prepare a list that exceeds the total funds available by 10%
    c. Prepare a list of books and include a list of alternate titles in case the ones on the first list aren't available
    d. Select a list of books and include the following line on the order, "Do Not Exceed This Amount" (the amount of the order)

Answer: d. Select a list of books and include the following line on the order, "Do Not Exceed This Amount" (the amount of the order)

Books can go in and out of print without warning, making it difficult to prepare a book order in the same way as one would prepare and equipment order. Instead of placing an order for the exact amount, it is best to create a list of books that goes well beyond the amount that needs to be spent. On the order form or purchase order write "Do Not Exceed" and list the maximum amount, including shipping and processing, that can be spent.

38. **When a book order is received, the first thing that should be done is:**
    (Skill 2.4) (Average Rigor)

    a. check the order against the invoice to make sure all items have been received
    b. catalog the books
    c. place the books on the shelves
    d. notify teachers that new books have arrived

Answer: a. check the order against the invoice to make sure all items have been received

As listed in question 37, it is difficult to create an exact order. If you have placed the order according to the guidelines in question 37 the first thing that must be done once an order is received is to check it against the invoice to make sure all shipped items have been received. It is also helpful to mark off the items received on the original order, making note of the items that are now out of print to avoid reordering those items.

LIBRARY MEDIA

TEACHER CERTIFICATION STUDY GUIDE

39. **A catalog that contains materials from several library collections is known as a:**
    (Skill 2.5) (Easy)

    a. shared catalog
    b. cooperative catalog
    c. union catalog
    d. universal catalog

Answer: c. union catalog

Option C is the most appropriate answer. A union catalog exists when various entities combine their resource lists so that they can be shown in one catalog. This is most often done throughout school districts or through partnerships with colleges and universities.

40. **The most efficient method of assessing which students are users or non-users of the library media center is reviewing:**
    (Skill 2.5) (Average Rigor)

    a. patron circulation records
    b. needs assessment surveys of students
    c. monthly circulation statistics
    d. the accession book for the current year

Answer: a. patron circulation records

By reviewing circulation records the school library media specialists can quickly survey who is and isn't checking out materials, making Option A the best answer. A needs assessment generally takes a good deal of time to complete. The monthly circulation records provide a snapshot of the number of books checked out during a specific period.

41. **OCLC is the acronym for:**
    (Skill 2.5) (Average Rigor)

    a. Online Computer Library Center
    b. Online Computer Library Catalog
    c. Online Computer Library Conference
    d. Online Computer Library Content

Answer: a. Online Computer Library Center

The most appropriate answer is Option A, the Online Computer Library Center. This center provides bibliographic (MARC) records.

42. In what area of a bibliographic record can the name of the author be found?
    (Skill 2.5) (Average Rigor)

    a. physical description area
    b. publication area
    c. terms of availability area
    d. title and statement of responsibility area

Answer: c. terms of availability

Terms of availability area is not part of the bibliographic record making Option C the most appropriate answer. The physical description includes details such as size and accompanying materials. The publication area defines the name of publisher and copyright day. The title and statement of responsibility area lists the title of the work, author, illustrator, and other pertinent information.

43. In MARC records the title information can be found under which tag?
    (Skill 2.5) (Rigorous)

    a. 130
    b. 245
    c. 425
    d. 520

Answer: b. 245

The 245 tag is where the title information is recorded in a MARC record. Option B is the most appropriate response. The 520 tag is where the summary is listed.

44. Which of the following is not a component of a bibliographic record?
    (Skill 2.5) (Rigorous)

    a. notes
    b. call number
    c. cover image
    d. physical description area

Answer: c. cover image

The cover image would be a detail listed under one of the components in a bibliographic record. It is not a component itself, making Option C the most appropriate response.

LIBRARY MEDIA

TEACHER CERTIFICATION STUDY GUIDE

45. **According to research on promotion techniques and support for library media programs, their staunchest ally must be the:**
    (Skill 2.6) (Easy)

    a. teaching faculty
    b. student body
    c. district media supervisor
    d. school principal

Answer: d. school principal

In order to make the necessary changes needed to make the school library media center the true learning center of the school the school library media specialist must have the full support of the principal. Moving to flexible scheduling and truly integrated learning can be a big adjustment. It is only with the vision and leadership of the school principal that any changes can occur.

46. **Which of the following are examples of ways to promote the school library media programs:**
    (Skill 2.6) (Easy)

    a. attend school board meetings
    b. serve on the school's curriculum committee
    c. invite school board members to media planning meetings
    d. all of the above

Answer: d. all of the above

Option D is the most appropriate answer. To promote the school library media program it is important that the media specialist attend school board meetings, serve on the school's curriculum committee and invite school board members and other officials to media planning meetings.

TEACHER CERTIFICATION STUDY GUIDE

47. All but which of the following criteria are used when determining fair use of copyrighted material for classroom use?
    (Skill 3.1) (Average Rigor)

    a. Brevity Test
    b. Spontaneity Test
    c. Time Test
    d. Cumulative Effect Test

Answer: c. Time Test

Copyrighted materials used in a classroom must pass the criteria under the brevity, spontaneity, and cumulative effect tests in order to fall under the fair use guidelines.

48. All of the following are periodical directories EXCEPT:
    (Skill 3.1) (Average Rigor)

    a. *Ulrich's*
    b. *TNYT*
    c. *SIRS*
    d. *PAIS*

Answer: b. TNYT

Option B is the most appropriate answer. All of the other directories listed are specifically for periodicals.

49. Which professional journal is published by the American Association of School Librarians?
    (Skill 3.1) (Average Rigor)

    a. *School Library Media Research*
    b. *Library Trends*
    c. *Library Power*
    d. *Voices of Youth Advocate*

Answer: a. *School Library Media Research*

The only journal listed that is published by the AASL is *School Library Media Research*. This makes Option A the most appropriate response.

TEACHER CERTIFICATION STUDY GUIDE

50. **All of the following should be housed in the reference collection EXCEPT:**
    (Skill 3.1) (Easy)

    a. atlas
    b. dictionary
    c. picture book
    d. collection of encyclopedias

    Answer: c. picture book

    While a picture book that is part of a special collection may be housed in a reference collection, normal picture books are not a part of the reference collection. Option C is the most appropriate answer.

51. **The Caldecott Medal was awarded to which book in 2002?**
    (Skill 3.2) (Rigorous)

    a. *The Three Pigs* by David Wiesner
    b. *Joseph Had a Little Overcoat* by Simms Taback
    c. *Golem* by David Wisniewski
    d. *Officer Buckle and Gloria* by Peggy Rathmann

    Answer: a. *The Three Pigs* by David Wiesner

    The correct answer is Option A. *Joseph Had a Little Overcoat* is the 2000 winner. *Golem* is the 1997 winner. *Officer Buckle and Gloria* is the 1996 winner.

52. **Which writer composes young adult literature in the fantasy genre?**
    (Skill 3.2) (Rigorous)

    a. Stephen King
    b. Piers Anthony
    c. Virginia Hamilton
    d. Phyllis Whitney

    Answer: b. Piers Anthony

    Piers Anthony is the author of such books as *Ghost*, *Firefly*, and *Bio of an Ogre*. He is the only author listed that writes fantasy for young adults.

TEACHER CERTIFICATION STUDY GUIDE

53. Which fiction genre do these authors represent: Isaac Asimov, Louise Lawrence, and Andre Norton?
    (Skill 3.2) (Rigorous)

    a. adventure
    b. romance
    c. science fiction
    d. fantasy

Answer: c. science fiction

All of these authors represent Option C. Science fiction titles for each include: Asimov – *I Robot, Foundation Trilogy*; Lawrence – *Children of the Dust, Moonwind*; Norton – *Stargate, Android at Arms*.

54. This award was first presented to its namesake in 1954. This bronze medal award honors an author or illustrator whose books were published in the United States and have made a lasting contribution to literature for children. This award is known as the:
    (Skill 3.2) (Rigorous)

    a. Newbery Medal
    b. Laura Ingalls Wilder Award
    c. Mildred L. Batchelder Award
    d. Carnegie Medal

Answer: b. Laura Ingalls Wilder Award

The most appropriate answer is Option B, the Laura Ingalls Wilder Award. The Newbery Medal Award honors the author who has made the most distinguished contribution to children's literature. The Batchelder Award was first presented in 1966 to the American publisher of a book first published in a foreign language. The Carnegie Medal is an award for excellence in children's videos.

TEACHER CERTIFICATION STUDY GUIDE

55. **All of the following are authors of young adult fiction EXCEPT:**
    (Skill 3.2) (Rigorous)

a. Paul Zindel
b. Norma Fox Mazer
c. S.E. Hinton
d. Maurice Sendak

Answer: d. Maurice Sendak

Maurice Sendak is best known for his picture books for young children such as *Where the Wild Things Are*.

56. **All of the following are authors of fantasy EXCEPT:**
    (Skill 3.2) (Rigorous)

a. Ray Bradbury
b. Ursula K. Le Guin
c. Piers Anthony
d. Ann McCaffrey

Answer: a. Ray Bradbury

The most appropriate answer is Option A. Ray Bradbury is a science fiction author and the others are fantasy writers.

57. **The award given for the best children's literature (text) is:**
    (Skill 3.2) (Easy)

a. the Caldecott Medal
b. the Newbery Medal
c. the Pulitzer
d. the Booklist

Answer: b. the Newbery Medal

Option B, the Newbery Medal Award, is the award give to an outstanding children's book. It was named for bookseller John Newbery, who was the first to publish literature for children in the second half of 18th century England. While the Caldecott Medal does recognize children's literature, this award is for outstanding illustrators.

TEACHER CERTIFICATION STUDY GUIDE

58. In recognition of outstanding translations of children's books this award was created in 1966. It is presented to the publisher that is responsible for translating the work into English.
    (Skill 3.2) (Rigorous)

    a. Newbery Medal
    b. Laura Ingalls Wilder Award
    c. Mildred L. Batchelder Award
    d. Carnegie Medal

Answer: c. Mildred L. Batchelder Award

The most appropriate answer is Option C. The Batchelder Award was first presented in 1966 to the American publisher of a book first published in a foreign language. The Newbery Medal honors the author who has made the most distinguished contribution to children's literature. The Carnegie Medal is an award for excellence in children's videos.

59. Which of the following file extensions does not represent an image file?
    (Skill 3.3) (Average Rigor)

    a. .jpeg
    b. .gif
    c. .csv
    d. .bmp

Answer: c. .csv

Image file types can be .jpeg or .jpg, .gif, .png, and .bmp to name a few. The .csv file stands for comma separated value and is usually associated with a spreadsheet. Other file types are .doc for word processed documents, .txt for text files, and .mdb or .db for database files.

LIBRARY MEDIA

60. **Which of the following has made the greatest impact on school library media centers in the last decade?**
    (Skill 3.3) (Average Rigor)

    a. censorship
    b. emerging technologies
    c. learning style research
    d. state funding reductions

Answer: b. emerging technologies

Advancements in technology have made the biggest impact in school library media centers during the last decade. These technologies have automated circulation, expanded available resources, and connected various locations through networks.

61. **USB is the acronym for:**
    (Skill 3.3) (Average Rigor)

    a. United Streaming Business
    b. Universal Serial Bus
    c. United Serial Business
    d. Universal Streaming Bus

Answer: b. Universal Serial Bus

Many computer peripherals are connected via the USB port on a computer. Many of these devices are self installing or plug and play devices. The most appropriate answer is Option B.

62. **A periodical index search that allows the user to pair keywords with and, but, or or is called:**
    (Skill 3.4) (Rigorous)

    a. Boolean
    b. dialoguing
    c. wildcarding
    d. truncation

Answer: a. Boolean

The most appropriate answer is Option A, Boolean. A Boolean search uses keywords along with terms such as and, but, and or, to define the search. Wildcarding is a form of searching that uses something such as an asterisk to find different formats of words or terms.

TEACHER CERTIFICATION STUDY GUIDE

63. A request from a social studies teacher for the creation of a list of historical fiction titles for a book report assignment is a _____ request.
    (Skill 3.4) (Rigorous)

    a. ready reference
    b. research
    c. specific needs
    d. complex search

    Answer: c. specific needs

    Requests made for particular titles or resources are known as a special needs request. Option C is the most appropriate answer.

64. Resources can be shared within a small geographic location such as a school by the use of a:
    (Skill 3.5) (Average Rigor)

    a. SWN
    b. MAN
    c. LAN
    d. WAN

    Answer: c. LAN

    A LAN or local area network allows users to share information within a small geographic area. The WAN or wide area network allows users to share information over a large geographic area.

65. All of the following are benefits of interlibrary loan EXCEPT:
    (Skill 3.5) (Rigorous)

    a. maximizing the use media center funds
    b. providing a wider range of resources available for patrons
    c. building partnerships with outside agencies
    d. eliminating the need for media assistants

    Answer: d. eliminating the need for media assistants

    The most appropriate response is Option D. Interlibrary loan allows the cooperating entities to maximize both funds and resources. It does not eliminate the need for media assistants.

LIBRARY MEDIA

TEACHER CERTIFICATION STUDY GUIDE

66. A network allows which of the following to occur?
    (Skill 3.5) (Average Rigor)

a. sharing files
b. sharing printers
c. sharing software
d. all of the above

Answer: d. all of the above

A network allows the sharing of files, printers, and software. This makes Option D the most appropriate response.

67. A group of students in the business club will be creating a website to sell their product. When selecting their domain name, which of the following extensions would be best to use?
    (Skill 3.6) (Rigorous)

a. .com
b. .edu
c. .cfm
d. .html

Answer: a. .com

A website that is used for commercial purposes should have a .com extension. The domain name is the location where the web page information is stored. Because the question specifically stated the domain name, Option A is the most appropriate answer. The .edu extension is used for educational institutions. The .html extension refers to the programming used to create a web page and stands for hypertext mark-up language..

68. An online database that provides print and electronic journal subscriptions is:
    (Skill 3.6) (Rigorous)

a. Kids Connect
b. KQWeb
c. EBSCO
d. NICEM

Answer: c. EBSCO

Option C, EBSCO is the most appropriate answer. It is an online database that provides print and electronic journals.

TEACHER CERTIFICATION STUDY GUIDE

69. Instruction provided via satellite or cable television is called:
    (Skill 3.7) (Average Rigor)

    a. home study
    b. distance learning
    c. extension services
    d. telecommunications

Answer: b. distance learning

To make the most of funding dollars many school districts have turned to courses offered via satellite, cable or online. Through these initiatives, students can have access to a wider array of courses that many small districts may not be able to fund. The most appropriate answer is Option B, distance learning.

70. Advantages of distance education include all of the following EXCEPT:
    (Skill 3.7) (Rigorous)

    a. students can access and respond to information outside of a normal schedule
    b. students have fewer choices regarding content
    c. homebound students may receive instruction
    d. it may be more cost effective to use distance learning than to hire a teacher

Answer: b. students have fewer choices regarding content

The use of distance learning classes actually expands the opportunities students have regarding content. The most appropriate answer is Option B.

71. The media specialist needs to expand the collection to include a wider variety of resources for visually impaired students. Which of the following would be least beneficial?
    (Skill 3.8) (Average Rigor)

    a. books with larger print
    b. books in Braille format
    c. books in audio format
    d. books in video format

Answer: d. books in video format

Books in video format would be least beneficial. Students with visual impairment would have a more difficult time gaining information from this format than any of the other formats listed.

LIBRARY MEDIA

TEACHER CERTIFICATION STUDY GUIDE

72. *Information Power: Building Partnerships for Learning* recommends flexible scheduling for:
    (Skill 3.9) (Easy)

    a. elementary school library media centers
    b. middle school library media centers
    c. secondary school library media centers
    d. all school library media centers

Answer: d. all school library media centers

Flexible access to resources is conducive to encouraging just-in-time learning. Resources are available at the point of need. Collaboration with classroom teachers makes flexible access even more effective. Thus all of the school library media centers should follow a flexible schedule making Option D the most appropriate answer.

73. When creating a schedule for a school library media center the type of schedule that maximizes access to resources is a:
    (Skill 3.9) (Easy)

    a. fixed schedule
    b. open schedule
    c. partial fixed schedule
    d. flexible schedule

Answer: d. flexible schedule
The best answer is d, flexible schedule. A flexible schedule allows students to have access to resources at the point of need. It maximizes the use of resources and allows media specialists to be accessible for collaborative planning with teachers.

TEACHER CERTIFICATION STUDY GUIDE

74. The school library media center should be an inviting space that encourages learning. To accomplish this, the school library media specialist should do all of the following EXCEPT:
(Skill 3.10) (Average Rigor)

   a. collaborate with school staff and students
   b. create a schedule where each class comes to the media center each week for instruction
   c. arrange materials so that they are easy to locate
   d. promote the program as a wonderful place for learning

Answer: b. create a schedule where each class comes to the media center each week for instruction

The goal of a school library is to operate under a flexible schedule to maximize use of the media center and its resources. This makes Option B the most appropriate answer.

75. A secondary school social studies teacher reads an article in the current month's *Smithsonian* that clarifies points in the unit of study on the day prior to the scheduled unit test. He asks the media specialist if copyright law would allow copying the entire 3100 word article for distribution to each student in his two honors American history classes. The media specialist's proper response is that:
(Skill 3.11) (Rigorous)

   a. he can make only one copy and read it to the class
   b. he may not copy it because of the word length
   c. he may excerpt sections of it to meet the brevity test
   d. he may copy the needed multiples, allowed by the spontaneity test

Answer: d. he may copy the needed multiples, allowed by the spontaneity test

Fair Use guidelines for nonprofit educational organizations does allow the copying and use of an entire article if it meets either the brevity or spontaneity test.

76. **Section 108 of the Copyright Act permits the copying of an entire book if three conditions are met. Which of the following is NOT one of those conditions?**
(Skill 3.11) (Rigorous)

a. the library intends to allow inter-library loan of the book
b. the library is an archival library
c. the copyright notice appears on all the copies
d. the library is a public library

Answer: a. the library intends to allow inter-library loan of the book

Section 108 does allow a library to make a single copy of a book for archival purposes. It does not cover books that are to be copied and used for inter-library loans.

77. **Under the copyright brevity test, an educator may reproduce without written permission:**
(Skill 3.11) (Rigorous)

a. 10% of any prose or poetry work
b. 500 words from a 5000 word article
c. 240 words of a 2400 word story
d. no work over 2500 words

Answer: b. 500 words from a 5000 word article

Under the brevity test up to 250 words of a poem can be copied providing it is under 2 pages. An article of 2500 words or less can be copied entirely. Ten percent of an article over 2500 words can be used making Option B the most appropriate answer.

TEACHER CERTIFICATION STUDY GUIDE

78. **Licensing has become a popular means of copyright protection in the area of:**
    (Skill 3.11) (Average Rigor)

    a. duplicating books for interlibrary loan
    b. use of software application on multiple machines
    c. music copying
    d. making transparency copies of books or workbooks that are too expensive to purchase

Answer: b. use of software application on multiple machines

When purchasing software the customer will generally received either a CD-ROM or DVD for installation purposes. The most important piece of packaging or file included on the software is the license. The license(s) purchased determine the number of computers in which the software can be loaded. Installing the software on more than the number listed on the license violated copyright and can result in a lawsuit by the publisher.

79. **"Fair Use" policy in videotaping off-air from commercial television requires:**
    (Skill 3.11) (Rigorous)

    a. material should be shown within 5 days and erased by the 20th day
    b. material should be shown within 10 days and erased by the 30th day
    c. material should be shown within 10 days and erased by the 45th day
    d. there are no restrictions

Answer: c. material should be shown within 10 days and erased by the 45th day

Fair Use Guidelines for recorded videotapes for nonprofit educational institutions state that the recording must be shown within 10 days and must be erased by the 45th day.

LIBRARY MEDIA

TEACHER CERTIFICATION STUDY GUIDE

80. The English I (9th Grade) teacher wants his students to become familiar with the contents of books in the reference area of the school library media center. He asks the library media specialist to recommend an activity to accomplish this goal. Which of the following activities would best achieve the goal?
    (Skill 4.1) (Average Rigor)

a. assign a research paper on a specific social issues topic
b. require a biography of a famous person
c. design a set of questions covering a variety of topics and initiate a scavenger hunt approach to their location
d. teach students the Dewey Decimal system and have them list several books in each Dewey subcategory

Answer: c. design a set of questions covering a variety of topics and initiate a scavenger hunt approach to their location

Students often learn best by doing. If the teacher's goal was for students to learn to use reference materials, then the best way to accomplish this is to design a task that does just that. In this case, the students are applying their knowledge making Option C the best answer.

81. Several Skills in *Information Skills ...* are worded exactly the same from K-12 because the students' mastery of the skill depends on performing that skill at ever advancing levels, even beyond graduation. Which of the following is one of those same worded skills?
    (Skill 4.1) (Rigorous)

a. examine award-winning materials
b. identify parts of a book
c. use materials without violating copyright laws
d. use appropriate sources to locate information

Answer: d. use appropriate sources to locate information

All students are expected to be able to use appropriate resources to find information. Therefore, the objective is worded the same from grades K-12 making Option D the most appropriate answer.

LIBRARY MEDIA

82. According to AASL/AECT guidelines, in her role as *instructional consultant,* the school library media specialist uses her expertise to:
   (Skill 4.1) (Average Rigor)

   a. assist teachers in acquiring information skills that they can incorporate into classroom instruction
   b. provide access to resource sharing systems
   c. plan lessons in media production
   d. provide staff development activities in equipment use

Answer: d. provide staff development activities in equipment use

As an instructional consultant, the school library media specialist does provide staff development activities. Providing access is part of the role of program administrator. Assisting teachers and planning lessons is part of the teaching role of a media specialist. This makes Option D the most appropriate answer.

83. An elementary teacher, planning a unit on the local environment, finds materials that are too global or above her students' ability level. The best solution to this problem is to:
   (Skill 4.1) (Rigorous)

   a. broaden the scope of the study to emphasize global concerns
   b. eliminate the unit from the content
   c. replace the unit with another unit that teaches the same skills
   d. have the students design their own study materials using media production techniques

Answer: d. have the students design their own study materials using media production techniques

When commercial materials cannot be found to meet student needs, the best alternative is to have students design their own materials. By designing and creating their own material, students tend to develop a deeper understanding of the subject.

84. **In assessing learning styles for staff development, consider that adults:**
    (Skill 4.1) (Rigorous)

a. are less affected by the learning environment than children
b. are more receptive to performing in and in front of groups
c. learn better when external motivations are guaranteed
d. demand little feedback

Answer: b. are more receptive to performing in and in front of groups

Adult learners often need as much feedback on performance as their students would especially when learning new skills. They are affected by their learning environments and will still perform even if there are no external rewards. It is Option B that is the correct answer. Adult learners are more receptive to performing in front of groups.

85. **A high school science teacher is about to begin a frog dissection unit. Three students refuse to participate. When asked for assistance, the library media specialist should:**
    (Skill 4.1) (Rigorous)

a. work with the teacher to design a replacement unit with print and non-print material on frog anatomy
b. offer to allow the student to use the library as a study hall during their class time
c. recommend that the student be sent to another class studying frogs without dissecting
d. abstain from condoning the student's refusal to work

Answer: a. work with the teacher to design a replacement unit with print and non-print material on frog anatomy

To ensure that students learn the material that would be covered by such an activity, there should be an alternate plan for instruction. The school library media specialist could play a crucial role in helping teachers to develop alternate plan. Option A is the best answer.

TEACHER CERTIFICATION STUDY GUIDE

86. **The most effective method of initiating closer contacts with and determining the needs of classroom teachers is to:**
    (Skill 4.2) (Average Rigor)

    a. ask to be included on the agenda of periodic faculty meetings
    b. present after school or weekend in-services in opening communication channels
    c. request permission to be included in grade-level or content-area meetings
    d. establish a library advisory committee with one representative from each grade level or content area

    Answer: c. request permission to be included in grade-level or content-area meetings

    Collaboration is a key component of any successful school library media program. By participating in grade level or content area meetings the media specialist can get a better idea of the specific needs of teachers

87. **To foster the collaborative process the media specialist must possess all of the following skills EXCEPT:**
    (Skill 4.2) (Easy)

    a. leadership
    b. flexibility
    c. perversity
    d. persistence

    Answer: c. perversity

    A school library media specialist must be flexible, possess good leadership skills, and be persistent, so Option C the most appropriate response.

88. **In most learning hierarchies, which of the following is the highest order critical thinking skill?**
    (Skill 4.3) (Average Rigor)

    a. appreciation
    b. inference
    c. recall
    d. comprehension

    Answer: a. appreciation

    In order of difficulty recall is the lowest critical thinking skill, followed by inference then comprehension and appreciation. Appreciation would be the highest level skill in this list, making Option A the most appropriate answer.

LIBRARY MEDIA

TEACHER CERTIFICATION STUDY GUIDE

89. **After reading *The Pearl,* a tenth grader asks, "Why can't we start sentences with *and* like John Steinbeck?" This student is showing the ability to:**
    (Skill 4.3) (Rigorous)

    a. appreciate
    b. comprehend
    c. infer
    d. evaluate

    Answer: d. evaluate

    Under the description of the Bloom's Taxonomy level of evaluation students that demonstrate this level of higher order thinking are able to:
    - Make choices based upon well thought out arguments
    - Compare ideas
    - And recognize subjectivity

90. **Howard Gardner created:**
    (Skill 4.3) (Easy)

    a. Multiple Intelligences
    b. Taxonomies of Learning
    c. Big6 Model
    d. @ Your Library

    Answer: a. Multiple Intelligences

    Howard Gardner is the creator of Multiple Intelligences. His theory stresses that each person has strengths is specific areas and that there are specific activities that will increase those strengths.

TEACHER CERTIFICATION STUDY GUIDE

91. A kindergarten class has just viewed a video on alligators. The best way to evaluate the suitability of the material for this age group is to:
(Skill 4.4) (Rigorous)

a. test the students' ability to recall the main points of the video
b. compare this product to other similar products on this content
c. observe the body language and verbal comments during the viewing
d. ask the children to comment on the quality of the video at the end of the viewing

Answer: c. observe the body language and verbal comments during the viewing

Students may be able to view any video and be able to recall facts, but suitability for a particular age may best be evaluated by how well students respond to the video as it is being viewed. This makes Option C the most appropriate answer.

92. Students' reading habits can be evaluated by use of which of the following:
(Skill 4.4) (Easy)

a. student surveys
b. interviews
c. standardized tests
d. all of the above

Answer: d. all of the above

Student surveys, interviews, and standardized tests can all be used to determine student reading habits making Option D the most appropriate answer.

93. Which of the following would be the best way to acclimate a media center volunteer to the workings of the media center is to:
(Skill 4.5) (Average Rigor)

a. provide the volunteer with a brochure regarding the workings of the media center
b. provide the volunteer with a manual that outlines their duties
c. provide a hands-on orientation session for the volunteer
d. provide a video for the volunteer that outlines their duties

Answer: c. provide a hands-on orientation session for the volunteer

Volunteers receive the greatest training benefit when they are provided with hands-on training. This makes Option C the most appropriate answer.

LIBRARY MEDIA

94. **As much as possible, information skills should be taught as:**
    (Skill 4.6) (Easy)

a. lessons independent of content studies
b. lessons to supplement content studies
c. lessons integrated into content studies
d. lessons enriched by content studies

Answer: c. lessons integrated into content studies

The current Information Literacy curriculum is thoroughly integrated into the core content areas. It stresses the correlation between the National Information Power Standards, Therefore, Option D is the correct answer.

95. **The creators of the Big6 Model are:**
    (Skill 4.6) (Average Rigor)

a. Eisenberg and Berkowitz
b. Marzano and Bloom
c. Bloom and Gardner
d. Lance and Eisenberg

Answer: a. Eisenberg and Berkowitz

The correct answer is Option A. Mike Eisenberg and Bob Berkowitz are the creators of the Big6 Model for developing Information Literacy Skills.

96. **When evaluating resources for effectiveness it is important to consider all of the following EXCEPT:**
    (Skill 4.7) (Average Rigor)

a. style of the web page.
b. the intended audience.
c. whether or not the site is from a scholarly source.
d. the scope of the information.

Answer: a. style of the web page

The style of the web page is not as important as who the audience is, whether or not the site is a scholarly source, and the scope of the information. This makes Option A the most appropriate answer.

TEACHER CERTIFICATION STUDY GUIDE

97. **Which of the following searches would most likely return the most results?**
    (Skill 4.7) (Average Rigor)

    a. lions and tigers
    b. lions not tigers
    c. lions or tigers
    d. lions and not tigers

Answer: c. lions or tigers

The use of OR in the search lets the search engine know to find articles that contain either of the words listed. With the use of AND, the search engine will look for articles that have both words in the article.

98. **The first step in planning a training program for untrained support staff is:**
    (Skill 5.1) (Rigorous)

    a. assessing the employee's existing skills
    b. identifying and prioritizing skills from the job description/evaluation instrument
    c. determining the time schedule for the completion of training
    d. studying the resume and speak to former employers.

Answer: b. identifying and prioritizing skills from the job description/evaluation instrument

The best place to begin planning a training program for untrained support staff is to take a look at the job description or evaluation instrument and determine the skills that need to be learned. From there one could study the employee's resume, assess their skills and plan a schedule for training

99. **Staff development activities in the use of materials and equipment are most effective if they:**
    (Skill 5.1) (Average Rigor)

    a. are conducted individually as need is expressed
    b. are sequenced in difficulty of operation or use
    c. result in use of the acquired skills in classroom lessons
    d. are evaluated for effectiveness

Answer: c. result in use of the acquired skills in classroom lessons

Option C is the most appropriate answer. The ultimate goal of most staff development activities is use or integration in the classroom.

LIBRARY MEDIA

100. Staff development is most effective when it includes:
    (Skill 5.1) (Average Rigor)

a. continuing support
b. hand-outs
c. video tutorials
d. stated objectives

Answer: a. continuing support

While the other options are important to consider when providing staff development, it is the provision of continuing support that ensures the information learned will used to its fullest potential. Option A is the most appropriate answer.

101. Which of the following is the most desirable learning outcome of a staff development workshop on *Teaching with Interactive DVDS*? Participants
    (Skill 5.1) (Average Rigor)

a. score 80% or better on a post-test
b. design content specific lessons from multiple resources
c. sign up to take additional workshops
d. encourage other teachers to participate in future workshops

Answer: b. design content specific lessons from multiple resources

The purpose of most staff development workshops is to foster integration of resources into the classroom. Performance and attendance in future workshops is desirable, but not the main goal.

102. Which of the following resources delineates eleven levels of involvement of the school library media center?
    (Skill 5.2) (Rigorous)

a. *Administering the School Library Media Center*
b. *Information Power*
c. *Taxonomies of the School Library Media Center*
d. *School Library Media Annual*

Answer: c. *Taxonomies of the School Library Media Center*

The most appropriate answer is Option C. The *Taxonomies of the School Library Media Center* delineates eleven levels of involvement.

103. All of the following organizations serve school libraries EXCEPT:
    (Skill 5.2) (Average Rigor)

    a. AASL
    b. AECT
    c. ALCT
    d. ALA

Answer: c. ALCT

The American Association of School Librarians (AASL), The Association for Educational Communications and Technology (AECT), and the American Library Association (ALA) are all organizations that support and serve school libraries.

104. National guidelines for school library media programs are generally developed by all of the following EXCEPT:
    (Skill 5.2) (Easy)

    a. AASL
    b. ALA
    c. AECT
    d. NECT

Answer: d. NECT

AASL, ALA, and AECT assist with developing guidelines for school library media centers. Option D is the most appropriate answer.

105. Which publication offers research based scholarly articles?
    (Skill 5.2) (Rigorous)

    a. *School Library Media Quarterly*
    b. *Media and Methods*
    c. *TechTrends*
    d. *Megatrends*

Answer: a. *School Library Media Quarterly*

School Library Media Quarterly is the only publication that publishes only research based articles.

106. IRA is the acronym for the:
    (Skill 5.3) (Easy)

a. Interactive Reading Administration.
b. International Reading Administration.
c. International Reading Association.
d. Interactive Reading Association.

Answer: c. International Reading Association

International Reading Association or IRA supports literacy and often partners with library associations.

107. All of the following are areas in which the school library media specialist supports the learning community EXCEPT:
    (Skill 5.4) (Average Rigor)

a. technician
b. collaboration
c. leadership
d. technology

Answer: a. technician

The school library media specialist should not have to serve in the capacity of a technician. They should work to collaborate with staff, provide leadership, and training on new technologies.

108. Current judicial rulings on censorship issues will most likely be discussed in:
    (Skill 5.5) (Average Rigor)

a. *Kirkus Reviews*
b. *School Library Media Review*
c. *New Media*
d. *Newsletter of Intellectual Freedom*

Answer: d. Newsletter of Intellectual Freedom.

Current judicial rulings and news on censorship can be found in The Newsletter of Intellectual Freedom. It is published by the American Library Association's Office of Intellectual Freedom.

TEACHER CERTIFICATION STUDY GUIDE

109. Which associations created the Library Bill of Rights and the Code of Ethics?
 (Skill 5.5) (Average Rigor)

 a. AASL and AECT
 b. ALA and AECT
 c. ALA and AASL
 d. ALA and NCTE

Answer: b. ALA and AECT

The American Library Association has created a Library Bill of Rights, while the Association of Educational Communications and Technology has designed a Code of Ethics.

110. A student looks for a specific title on domestic violence. When he learns it is overdue, he asks the library media specialist to tell him the borrower's name. The library media specialist should first:
 (Skill 5.5) (Rigorous)

 a. readily reveal the borrower's name
 b. suggest he look for the book in another library
 c. offer to put the boy's name on reserve pending the book's return
 d. offer to request an interlibrary loan

Answer: c. offer to put the boy's name on reserve pending the book's return

Patron confidentiality is of the utmost importance. The media specialist also needs to meet the needs of the patron requesting the book. The most appropriate course of action is Option C, offer to put the boy's name on reserve pending the book's return.

111. **Freedom of access of information for children includes all of the following EXCEPT:**
(Skill 5.5) (Average Rigor)

a. development of critical thinking
b. reflection of social growth
c. provision for religious differences
d. discrimination of different points of view

Answer: c. provision for religious differences

The Freedom of Access of Information for children does not include provisions for religious differences making Option C the best answer. It does provide for freedom to form and express opinions.

112. **The Library Bill of Rights includes all of the following EXCEPT:**
(Skill 5.5) (Average Rigor)

a. information presented in a library should be selected based upon the age level of the students
b. resources should include a representation of all ideas, concepts, and backgrounds
c. resources should not be excluded because of viewpoint
d. censorship should be challenged

Answer: a. information presented in a library should be selected based upon the age level of the students

Libraries should work to provide as much access to resources as possible. Resources should not be selected solely based upon age level of students. This makes Option A the most appropriate answer.

113. **AECT's Code of Ethics contains which of the following sections?**
(Skill 5.5) (Average Rigor)

a. Commitment to Media
b. Commitment to Education
c. Commitment to Society
d. Commitment to School

Answer: c. Commitment to Society

There are four sections found in AECT's Code of Ethics: Preamble, Commitment to Individual, Commitment to Society, Commitment to Profession. This makes Option C the most appropriate answer.

114. The Right to Read Statement was issued by:
    (Skill 5.5) (Rigorous)

    a. AECT
    b. ALA
    c. NCTE
    d. NICEM

Answer: c. NCTE

The National Council of Teachers of English (NCTE) is responsible for the creation of the Right to Read Statement. This make Option C the most appropriate answer.

115. Instructional materials are evolving into all of the following formats EXCEPT:
    (Skill 5.6) (Easy)

    a. ebooks
    b. online magazines
    c. audio cassettes
    d. interactive software

Answer: c. audio cassettes

Audio cassettes are or have given way to newer formats such as CD-ROMs and mp3 files. This makes Option C the most appropriate response.

116. Current trends in school library media include all of the following EXCEPT:
    (Skill 5.6) (Easy)

    a. collaboration
    b. face-to-face instruction
    c. flexible scheduling
    d. technology integration

Answer: b. face-to-face instruction

Face-to-face instruction is not one of the current trends in school library media. Collaboration, flexible scheduling, and technology integration are some of the trends affecting school library media programs.

TEACHER CERTIFICATION STUDY GUIDE

117. **Which of the following is part of the American Library Association's Advocacy Toolkit?**
(Skill 5.7) (Easy)

a. @ Your Library
b. Code of Ethics
c. Information Power
d. Taxonomies of Learning

Answer: a. @ Your Library

The American Library Association's Advocacy Toolkit provides libraries with resources to promote their library programs. @Your Library is a part of that toolkit.

118. **This outlines the role of the school library media specialist and the programs they manage.**
(Skill 5.7) (Average Rigor)

a. Taxonomies of Learning
b. Code of Ethics
c. @ Your Library
d. Library Bill of Rights

Answer: c. @ Your Library

As part of ALA's Advocacy Toolkit, @ Your Library outlines the role of the school library media specialist and the programs they manage. This makes Option C the most appropriate response.

119. Must have been teaching for three years, hold a bachelor's degree and have a valid teaching license are eligibility requirements for:
(Skill 5.8) (Easy)

a. Library Media Specialist
b. Curriculum Specialist
c. National Board Certification
d. none of the above

Answer: c. National Board Certification

One option open to currently certified school library media specialists it to pursue National Board Certification in Library Media. To be eligible for national board certification one must have been teaching for three years, hold a bachelor's degree and have a valid teaching license. Obtaining National Board Certification is one of the highest symbols of educational achievement.

120. A school with 500–749 students should have how many media specialists?
(Skill 5.8) (Easy)

a. 1 part-time media specialist
b. 1 full time media specialist
c. 2 full time media specialist
d. no media specialist required

Answer: b. 1 full time media specialist

It is recommended that schools with 500 to 749 students have at least 1 full time media specialist. This makes Option B the most appropriate response.

TEACHER CERTIFICATION STUDY GUIDE

121. **Which of the following is the best description of the ALA recommendations for certification for a school library media specialist?**
(Skill 5.8) (Rigorous)

   a. a bachelor's degree in any content area plus 30 hours of library/information science
   b. a master's degree from an accredited Educational Media program
   c. a bachelor's degree in library/information science and a master's degree in any field of education
   d. a master's degree from an accredited Library and Information Studies program

Answer: d. a master's degree from an accredited Library and Information Studies Program

According to the American Library Association to become a certified school librarian one should attain a master's degree from and ALA accredited Library and Information Studies Program. It is important to check a program's accreditation status before pursuing a degree at that institution. Some locations will not hire librarians who did not graduate from an accredited program.

122. **The federal law enacted by Congress in December 2000 that imposed specific Internet restrictions on schools that receive Federal E-rate funding is known as:**
(Skill 5.9) (Average Rigor)

   a. CIP
   b. CIPA
   c. SIP
   d. AUP

Answer: b. CIPA

The Children's Internet Protection Act (CIPA) specifies that schools or libraries that receive Federal E-rate funding must enact certain guidelines such as Internet filters and monitoring software.

TEACHER CERTIFICATION STUDY GUIDE

123. When a parent complains about the content of a specific title in a library media collection, the library media specialist's first course of action in responding to the complaint is to:
    (Skill 5.9) (Rigorous)

    a. remove the title from the shelf and purge it from both the catalog and the shelf list
    b. place the book in reserve status for circulation at parent request only
    c. submit the complaint to a district review committee
    d. explain the principles of intellectual freedom to the complaining parent

Answer: d. explain the principles of intellectual freedom to the complaining parent

Following the Library Bill of Rights and the principles of Intellectual Freedom, the primary mission of a school library media program is to provide access to information without censorship. Therefore Option D is the best answer.

124. Funded under the No Child Left Behind Act, this program helps LEAs improve reading achievement by providing increased access to up-to-date school library materials including technologically advanced school library media centers and professionally certified school library media specialists.
    (Skill 5.9) (Rigorous)

    a. 21st Century Schools
    b. Improving Literacy Through School Libraries
    c. @ Your Library
    d. Technology in the 21st Century

Answer: b. Improving Literacy Through School Libraries

Improving Literacy Through School Libraries is funded under Title I, Part B, Subpart 4 of the Elementary and Secondary Education Act.

LIBRARY MEDIA

125. **In the landmark U.S. Supreme Court ruling in favor of Pico, the court's opinion established that:**
    (Skill 5.9) (Rigorous)

a. library books, being optional not required reading, could not be arbitrarily removed by school boards
b. school boards have the same jurisdiction over library books as they have over textbooks
c. the intent to remove pervasively vulgar material is the same as the intent to deny free access to ideas
d. First Amendment challenges in regards to library books are the responsibility of appeals courts

Answer: a. library books, being optional not required reading, could not be arbitrarily removed by school boards

In the Supreme Court Case *Board of Education, Island Trees Union Free School District No. 26 v. Pico* states that library books, being optional not required reading, could not be arbitrarily removed by school boards.

WEB RESOURCES

Association for Educational Computing and Technology. "Association for Educational Communications and Technology." *Association for Educational Computing and Technology*. 2001. September 2, 2007. http://www.aect.org/default.asp .

Association for Educational Computing and Technology. "Code of Ethics." *About AECT: Code of Ethics*. 2006. September 8, 2007. http://www.aect.org/About/Ethics.asp.

American Library Association. "Information Power Because Student Achievement is the Bottom Line." *American Association of School Librarians*. July 10, 2006. August 28, 2007. http://www.ala.org/ala/aasl/aaslproftools/informationpower/informationpower.cfm.

American Library Association. "Budget and Finance." *American Library Association Professional Tools*. 2007. August 28, 2007. http://www.ala.org/Template.cfm?Section=budgeting.

American Library Association. "American Association of School Librarians." *American Association of School Librarians*. 2007. September 2, 2007. http://www.ala.org/ala/aasl/aaslindex.cfm.

American Library Association. "American Library Association." *American Library Association*. 2007. September 2, 2007. www.ala.org.

American Library Association. "Intellectual Freedom Statements and Policies." *American Library Association Statements and Policies*. 2007. September 2, 2007. http://www.ala.org/ala/oif/statementspols/statementspolicies.htm.

American Library Association. "AASL Resource Guides for School Library Media Program Development Flexible Scheduling." *American Association for School Librarians: Flexible Scheduling*. 2007. September 2, 2007. http://www.ala.org/ala/aasl/aaslproftools/resourceguides/flexiblescheduling.cfm.

American Library Association. "ALA Equipment and Facilities Management." *American Library Association Professional Tools*. 2007. September 2, 2007. http://www.ala.org/Template.cfm?Section=equipment.

American Library Association. "ALA Workbook for Selection Policy Writing." *American Library Association Professional Tools*. 2007. September 2, 2007. http://www.ala.org/Template.cfm?Section=dealing&Template=/ContentManagement/ContentDisplay.cfm&ContentID=164386 .

American Library Association. "ALA Library Fact Sheet 15: Weeding Library Collections: A Selected Annotated Bibliography for Library Collection Evaluation." *American Library Association Library Fact Sheet.* 2007. September 2, 2007.
http://www.ala.org/ala/alalibrary/libraryfactsheet/fact15.cfm.

American Library Association. "Library Bill of Rights." *American Library Association.* 2007. September 2, 2007.
http://www.ala.org/ala/oif/statementspols/statementsif/librarybillrights.htm.

American Library Association. "Welcome to the Newbery Medal Home Page." *Awards and Scholarships.* 2007. September 7, 2007.
http://www.ala.org/Template.cfm?Section=bookmediaawards&template=/ContentManagement/ContentDisplay.cfm&ContentID=149311

American Library Association. "Welcome to the Caldecott Medal Home Page." *Awards and Scholarships.* 2007. September 7, 2007.
http://www.ala.org/Template.cfm?Section=bookmediaawards&template=/ContentManagement/ContentDisplay.cfm&ContentID=164637

American Library Association. "Book/Media Awards." *Awards and Scholarships.* 2007. September 7, 2007.
http://www.ala.org/Template.cfm?Section=bookmediaawards

American Library Association. "Interlibrary Loans." *ALA Library Fact Sheet 8: Interlibrary Loan.* 2007. September 7, 2007.
http://www.ala.org/ala/alalibrary/libraryfactsheet/alalibraryfactsheet8.cfm

American Library Association. "Federal Law—Americans With Disabilities Act." *ADA.* 2007. September 7, 2007.
http://www.ala.org/ala/washoff/contactwo/oitp/emailtutorials/accessibilitya/03.cfm

American Library Association. "Issues and Advocacy." *American Association of School Librarians*. 2007. September 7, 2007.
http://www.ala.org/ala/aasl/aaslissues/issuesadvocacy.cfm

American Library Association. "21st Century Literacy @ Your Library." *Professional Tools*. 2007. September 7, 2007.
http://www.ala.org/ala/proftools/21centurylit/21stcenturyliteracy.htm

American Library Association. "Advocacy Resource Center." *Issues and Advocacy*. 2007. September 7, 2007.
http://www.ala.org/ala/issues/issuesadvocacy.htm

Association of College and Research Libraries. "Guidelines for Distance Learning Library Services." *Guidelines for Distance Learning Library Services.* May 1, 2007. September 8, 2007.
http://www.ala.org/ala/acrl/acrlstandards/guidelinesdistancelearning.cfm

Big6 Associates. "Big6: Information Skills for Student Achievement." *Big6: An Information Problem-Solving Process.* August 31, 2007. September 8, 2007.
http://www.big6.com

Daniel, Evelyn. "Two Taxonomies of the School Library Media Program." *Two Taxonomies of the School Library Media Program.* January 31, 2002. September 2, 2007. http://www.ils.unc.edu/daniel/242/Taxonomies.html

FranklinCovey. "FranklinCovey Mission Statement Builder." *Library and Resources.* 2007. August 28, 2007.
http://www.franklincovey.com/fc/library_and_resources/mission_statement_builder

Furrie, Betty. "Understanding MARC." *Understanding MARC.* 2003. September 2, 2007. http://www.loc.gov/marc/umb/

Gardner, Howard. "Multiple Intelligences." *Howard Gardner Professor of Cognition and Education Harvard Graduate School of Education.* 2006. September 6, 2007. http://www.howardgardner.com/MI/mi.html

Glaister, Bill. "Our Favorite Children's and Young Adult Authors (Arranged by Genre)." *Curriculum Laboratory*. August, 2007. September 7, 2007. http://www.uleth.ca/edu/currlab/handouts/genres.html

Google. "Google Directory of Book Jobbers." *Google Directory*. 2007. September 2, 2007. http://www.google.com/Top/Business/Information_Services/Library_Services/Book_Jobbers/

Instructional Technology Division, NC DPI. "Collaboration Toolkit." *IMPACT: Guidelines for North Carolina Media and Technology Programs*. 2006. September 1, 2007. http://www.ncwiseowl.org/impact/toolkit.htm

Instructional Technology Division, NC DPI. "Program Administration." *IMPACT: Guidelines for Media and Technology Programs*. 2006. September 1, 2007. http://www.ncwiseowl.org/Impact/progAdmin.htm#mtac

Internet Tutorials. "Boolean Searching on the Internet." *Internet Tutorials*. August, 2007. September 7, 2007. http://www.internettutorials.net/boolean.html

Library of Congress. "Library of Congress Classification Outline." *Library of Congress*. September 1, 2007. http://www.loc.gov/catdir/cpso/lcco

Loertscher, David V. "Collection Mapping in the LMC." *Collection Mapping*. 1996. September 2, 2007. http://www.lmcsource.com/pdfs/CollectionMapping.pdf

National Board for Professional Teaching Standards. "Library Media/Early Childhood Through Young Adulthood." *National Board for Professional Teaching Standards*. 2007. September 8, 2007. http://www.nbpts.org/the_standards/standards_by_cert?ID=19&x=47&y=13

National Council of Teachers of English. "The Student's Right to Read." *NCTE Guideline*. 1981. September 8, 2007. www.ncte.org/about/over/positions/level/gen/107616.htm

National Education Association. "National Education Association." *National Education Association*. 2007. September 2, 2007. http://www.nea.org/index.html

Purdue University. "Welcome to Purdue OWL (online writing lab) Research and Citation Link." *The OWL at Purdue*. 2007. September 2, 2007. http://owl.english.purdue.edu/owl

Read, Elizabeth. "AACR2: Access Points." *Queen's Library University*. January 6, 2005. September 2, 2007. http://130.15.161.74/techserv/cat/Sect02a/c02a2.html

SirsiDynix. "Long-Range Library Planning." *Library HQ*. August 28, 2007. http://www.libraryhq.com/plans.html

Trochim, William M. K. "Types of Data." *Research Methods Database*. 2006. August 28, 2007. http://www.socialresearchmethods.net/kb/datatype.php

United States Copyright Offices. "Copyright." *U. S. Copyright Office – Fair Use*. August 25, 2007. September 8, 2007. http://www.copyright.gov/fls/fl102.html

Wikipedia. "List of Dewey Decimal Classification." *List of Dewey Decimal Classification*. August 14, 2007. September 2, 2007. http://en.wikipedia.org/wiki/List_of_Dewey_Decimal_Classes

Wikipedia. "International Standard Bibliographic Description." *International Standard Bibliographic Description*. September 7, 2007. September 7, 2007. http://en.wikipedia.org/wiki/International_Standard_Bibliographic_Description

Wikipedia. "Computer Network." *Computer Network*. September 8, 2007. September 8, 2007. http://en.wikipedia.org/wiki/Computer_network

Wilson, H. W. "Sears List of Subject Headings 18th Edition." *H. W. Wilson*. 2007. September 7, 2007. http://www.hwwilson.com/print/searslst_18th.cfm

XAMonline, INC. 21 Orient Ave. Melrose, MA 02176

Toll Free number 800-509-4128

TO ORDER Fax 781-662-9268 OR www.XAMonline.com

WEST SERIES

PO#　　　　　　　Store/School:

Address 1:

Address 2 (Ship to other):

City, State Zip

Credit card number_____-_____-_____-_____　expiration_____

EMAIL _____

PHONE　　　　　　　　　　FAX

ISBN	TITLE	Qty	Retail	Total
978-1-58197-638-0	WEST-B Basic Skills			
978-1-58197-609-0	WEST-E Biology 0235			
978-1-58197-693-9	WEST-E Chemistry 0245			
978-1-58197-566-6	WEST-E Designated World Language: French Sample Test 0173			
978-1-58197-557-4	WEST-E Designated World Language: Spanish 0191			
978-1-58197-614-4	WEST-E Elementary Education 0014			
978-1-58197-636-6	WEST-E English Language Arts 0041			
978-1-58197-634-2	WEST-E General Science 0435			
978-1-58197-637-3	WEST-E Health & Fitness 0856			
978-1-58197-635-9	WEST-E Library Media 0310			
978-1-58197-674-8	WEST-E Mathematics 0061			
978-1-58197-556-7	WEST-E Middle Level Humanities 0049, 0089			
978-1-58197-043-2	WEST-E Physics 0265			
978-1-58197-563-5	WEST-E Reading/Literacy 0300			
978-1-58197-552-9	WEST-E Social Studies 0081			
978-1-58197-639-7	WEST-E Special Education 0353			
978-1-58197-633-5	WEST-E Visual Arts Sample Test 0133			
	SUBTOTAL		Ship	$8.25
	FOR PRODUCT PRICES VISIT WWW.XAMONLINE.COM		TOTAL	

www.ingramcontent.com/pod-product-compliance
Lightning Source LLC
Chambersburg PA
CBHW080539300426
44111CB00017B/2804